*The Gromacki
Expository Series*

Stand Bold
in Grace

*An Exposition of
Hebrews*

Dr. Robert Gromacki

An Exposition
of
Hebrews

Stand
Bold
in Grace

Kress Christian
PUBLICATIONS

The Gromacki
Expository Series

Published by:
Kress Christian Publications
P.O. Box 132228
The Woodlands, TX 77393

All Scripture quotations, unless otherwise indicated, are from the *King
James Version* of the Bible.

ISBN 0-9717568-7-2

Cover Design: D.M. Batterman, R&D Design Services

To my
son-in-law
David John Lawhead

Contents

Preface

The modern church is much like ancient Israel. The old covenant people wanted to be delivered from their bondage in Egypt, but they did not want to follow Moses into the Promised Land. They just marked time wandering in the wilderness.

In like manner many Christians are happy that they have been saved from the judgment of hell, but they refuse to trust God for the abundant life in their daily experience. They simply survive in their immaturity, carnality, and mediocrity.

In the Book of Hebrews, the author exhorts his readers to advance into the full blessings of the new covenant. He wants them to enjoy the total ministry of Jesus Christ in this life. He warns them about the dire consequences for rejecting the provision and leadership of the Savior.

This study has been designed to teach the Word of God to others. It is an attempt to make clear the meaning of the English text (King James Version) through organization, exposition, and careful use of the Greek text. It is a readable study, using a nontechnical vocabulary and smooth transitions from one section to the next. The words of the English text are in quotation marks for easy reference, the Greek words are transliterated, and necessary grammatical explanations are in footnotes. This study also contains a wealth of cross-references to other supporting passages of Scripture.

Divided into thirteen chapters, this book can be used by adult Sunday school classes or Bible study groups for a traditional quarter of thirteen weeks. Concluding each chapter are discussion questions, designed to stimulate personal inquiry and to make the truth of God relevant. This book can also be used as a private Bible study guide by both the pastor and the layman. In all situations, however, this book should be read with an open Bible in front of the student. It is my prayer that men and women will be blessed and edified as they undertake this study of Hebrews.

This volume will complement my other expositions published by Baker Book House: *Called to be Saints* (I Corinthians), *Stand Firm in the Faith* (II Corinthians), *Stand Fast in Liberty* (Galatians), *Stand United in Joy* (Philippians), *Stand Perfect in Wisdom* (Colossians and Philemon), and *Stand True to the Charge* (I Timothy).

A special word of thanks is extended to Cornelius Zylstra and Dan Van't Kerkhoff, editors at Baker Book House, who assisted me in this project.

Also, my love and appreciation go to my dear wife Gloria, who carefully typed the manuscript.

Introduction

I. WRITER

Who wrote Hebrews? This question has puzzled believers for generations. Although the name is not indicated, the writer was definitely known to his readers.[1] Even though there is frequent quotation of the Old Testament,[2] not once did the author refer to any biblical writer by name. In order to remain consistent within his literary style, the author perhaps chose to remain anonymous. In this way his readers would be motivated by the impact of his message rather than by the influence of his personality or position.

Scholars have suggested several names as possibilities for the authorship of this book. Among them are Apollos, Barnabas, Luke, Priscilla, Silas, and, of course, Paul. Generally, the debate centers around Paul: Did he or did he not write the book? Quite often, more effort is spent in the denial of Pauline authorship than in the positive affirmation of arguments for a substitute writer. Even the early church had problems over the authenticity of the book. The Eastern church accepted it as an original Pauline, canonical book, whereas the Western church denied its Pauline authorship and excluded it from the canon, mainly because of the uncertain authorship.

What, then, are the arguments used against the view that Paul wrote the book? Since Paul opened all thirteen of his epistles

1. This situation is not unique because many biblical books do not contain the name of the author: the Gospels, John's epistles, and several Old Testament books.
2. Second only to Revelation in the New Testament.

11

with a salutation including his name, the absence both of his name and the salutation is first cited (cf. II Thess. 3:17). The critics also claim that the literary style which undergirds Hebrews is substantially different from that in acknowledged Pauline writings. Since Paul was the self-acknowledged Apostle to the Gentiles (Acts 9:15; Gal. 2:7), would he have written such a lengthy treatise to a Jewish assembly? Paul claimed that his message and apostleship were given to him directly by Christ (Gal. 1:1, 11–12), but this writer was dependent upon others for his knowledge of salvation: "How shall we escape, if we neglect so great salvation; which at the first began to be spoken by the Lord, and was confirmed unto us by them that heard him?" (2:3). Like Luke, he seemed to identify himself as a second-generation Christian (cf. Luke 1:1–2). The central theme of the book, the high priesthood of Christ, is not anywhere explained in Paul's writings. The quotations of the Old Testament are all taken from the Septuagint, whereas Paul generally quoted from both the Greek translation and the Hebrew Old Testament. Timothy's release probably took place after the writing of II Timothy or after Paul's martyrdom (13:23; cf. II Tim. 4:9, 21). Since the book was probably written just before the destruction of the Jerusalem temple (A.D. 70) or in the latter third of the first century, the author's expectation of a release from imprisonment does not fit into the political atmosphere of Paul's second Roman captivity (10:34; 13:23; cf. II Tim. 4:6). Honest inquiry must admit that these arguments considered together do appear impressive.

On the other side, what are the proofs cited to support the Pauline authorship of this book? The author was in prison, and Paul suffered many imprisonments (10:34; cf. II Cor. 11:23). This one does not have to be equated with his second Roman captivity. In all previous confinements he did expect to be released (13:23; cf. Phil. 2:23–24; Philem. 22). Contrary to critical analysis, there are several doctrinal affinities between Hebrews and Paul's writings: the preeminence of Christ (1:1–3; cf. Col. 1:14–19); the authentication of apostles by divine gifts and miracles (2:3–4; cf. I Cor. 12–14; II Cor. 12:12); the humiliation of Christ (2:9–18; cf. Phil. 2:5–11); the use of Israel's wanderings as examples to contemporary believers (3:7—4:8; cf. I Cor. 10:1–11); the temporary nature of the old covenant (8:1–13; cf. II Cor. 3:6–18); and the emphasis of the faith principle (11:1–40; cf. Rom. 1:17). In fact, Habakkuk's declaration that the just shall live by faith (Hab. 2:4) is quoted three times in the New Testament (Heb. 10:38; cf. Rom. 1:17; Gal. 3:11). This quotation seems to have been a distinctive Pauline trait. The close companionship of Timothy is also cited (13:23). Although Paul saw himself as an apostle to the Gentiles, he preached to the Jews first wherever he went (Rom. 1:16), often visited the Jerusalem church, and had a deep spiritual concern for Israel (Rom. 9:1–5; 10:1–4). His Pharisaical training under Gamaliel in Jerusalem would have provided him with a thorough knowledge of the history and the rites of the Jewish sacrificial system (Acts 22:30). Few others would have had the background to compose such a book heavy with allusions to Exodus and Leviticus. The closing section bears a great resemblance to Pauline concerns. He requested prayer in his behalf (13:18; cf. Eph. 6:19), desired a good conscience (13:18; cf. Acts 24:16; II Tim. 1:3), identified the Father as the God of peace (13:20; cf. Rom. 15:33; Phil. 4:9; I Thess. 5:23), and pronounced a benediction of grace (13:25; cf. Philem. 25). Some have even suggested that Peter's allusion to Paul's writings includes a specific reference to Hebrews (II Peter 3:15–16).[3]

What conclusions can be drawn from this debate? In the final analysis, only God knows for sure who the author is. Although the book is nameless, this fact does not detract from the authenticity or inspired authority of its contents. If the book was not written by Paul, then it must have been composed by a close associate of the apostle with or without his direct supervision.

3. Since Peter was an apostle to the Jews, he probably wrote to Jewish Christians (I Peter 1:1; cf. Acts 2:9–11; 8:1–4). The phrase "written unto you" (II Peter 3:15) thus would refer to a letter written to Jewish Christians. Only Hebrews would qualify.

II. RECIPIENTS OF THE LETTER

To whom did the author write? The answer to this important question will help solve many of the interpretative problems within the book. Were they saved? Unsaved? Did the author think that they were saved but in reality they were not? Where did they live?

First of all, he regarded his readers as believers. He addressed them as "brethren" (3:1, 12) and as "beloved" (6:9). To him, they were "partakers of the heavenly calling" (3:1) and "partakers of Christ" (3:14). The warnings given to them would only apply to genuine believers (3:12-13). Unbelievers are already possessed with an evil heart of unbelief; nowhere are they commanded to exhort each other.

Second, they were immature (5:11-14). They had been saved a long time, but they had not grown spiritually. They were unable to receive the meat of biblical teaching because they were on a milk diet. They did not have enough knowledge or experience to make adult distinctions between right and wrong choices. The writer saw them as spiritual "babes."

Third, they were wavering in their faith. After their conversion, they had endured persecutions, identified themselves with other oppressed believers, seen their material possessions destroyed, and had compassion over the author's imprisonment (10:32-34). However, their present conduct did not manifest that initial freshness and joy any more. They grew tired of their persecutions and failed to trust God as they once did (10:35-38).

Fourth, they were apparently well known to the author. He planned to visit them after his release from prison (13:23). In the hope of his restoration to them (13:19), there is a hint that he had been with them at least on one occasion before.

Fifth, the readers either resided in Rome or in Palestine. In his closing salutation, he wrote: "They of Italy salute you" (13:24). Does this mean that the author was in Italy, perhaps Rome, and that the Italian believers wanted to send greetings? Or, does it mean that Italian believers, outside of their homeland, wanted to be remembered to their Christian friends back

in Italy?[4] Evangelical opinion is divided over the issue. Advocates of a Roman destination point out that the readers were
known for their financial generosity (6:10) whereas the church
at Jerusalem was marked by poverty (Acts 11:27–30; Rom.
15:26). However, the Jerusalem believers did unselfishly share
their material possessions (Acts 2:44–45; 4:32–37). Even the
Macedonian churches were known paradoxically for both their
poverty and liberality (II Cor. 8:1–2). If the readers' knowledge
of the sacrificial rites came from a past participation in temple
worship at Jerusalem, then they were probably residents of the
environs around the Holy City; however, as loyal pilgrims to the
annual feasts of Passover, Pentecost, or Tabernacles (cf. Acts
2:10), they could have gained their facts through that experience. If their knowledge was based solely upon a study of the
Old Testament, then they probably resided outside of Palestine.
In conclusion, no one can really be dogmatic about the exact
destination.

III. TIME AND PLACE

As indicated before, the readers had been saved for a rather
long period of time (5:12). They had been verbally assaulted and
had suffered the loss of personal property for their faith, but
they had not yet been beaten or killed (12:3–4). However, the
threat of such severe persecution now loomed in their immediate future. It may be that the imminent Jewish–Roman war
prompted this threat. As Jewish Christians they faced a personal
dilemma. Should they identify themselves racially with their
fellow Jews in possible combat against the Romans and thus
gain the favor of their countrymen? Or, should they remain
identified with the Jewish–Gentile Christian assembly and as-
sume a neutral position politically, especially since Christ predicted the destruction of Jerusalem with its temple because of
her rejection of Him (Matt. 23:37—24:1-2)? This latter action
would incur the wrath of their fellow Jews. They thus faced this

4. Grammatically, the preposition *apo,* translated "of," seems to support the
second view.

question: Shall we go on with Christ and His people even though it means persecution and possible death, or shall we go back to be identified with Jewish national and religious life again and thus avoid this persecution? Some had already made their decision and had defected from the Christian assembly (10:25). The majority had not yet made up their minds. The author, aware of the situation, wrote to admonish them not to take this drastic step of disobedience but to endure patiently and faithfully the persecutions while they anticipated both the imminent coming of Christ and the destruction of Jerusalem and its temple (10:22–25).

There is good evidence that the book was written just a few years before the destruction of Jerusalem (A.D. 70), perhaps about A.D. 67–68. It had to be composed during the lifetime of second-generation Christians who themselves had been saved for some while (2:3–4; 5:11–14). Timothy was still alive (13:23). The author uses present verbal tenses and participles to describe the ritual service of the priests (8:4, 13; 9:4, 5, 9; 10:1, 8, 11; 13:10, 11). This would seem to indicate that the temple was still standing. However, some have pointed out that the use of the present tense was only a literary device, and it was employed by church fathers writing after A.D. 70. They further claim that the author was comparing the priestly ministry of Christ with that of the Mosaic tabernacle, not that of the Zerubbabel–Herod temple. The natural reading of the text, though, seems to refer to a comparison of simultaneous ministries on earth and in heaven. If the book had been written after A.D. 70, certainly the author would have referred to the destruction of the temple as his capstone argument. His silence argues for the earlier date.

IV. PURPOSES

The main purpose was to demonstrate the superiority of the person and work of Christ to the Old Testament sacrificial system (1:1—10:18). Once the author had made that point, he was then able to combat the imminent danger of defection (2:1-4; 10:19-25), to provoke his readers to growth into Christian maturity (5:11-14; 10:32-39), to comfort them in their persecutions (11:1—12:13), to warn them about the severity of divine chastisement (6:3-12; 10:26-31; 12:3-13), to alert them to the dangers of false teaching (13:9), and to request prayer for himself (13:18-25).

V. DISTINCTIVE FEATURES

This book contains the classic presentation of the doctrine of the priesthood of Christ. Although other books emphasize the value of Christ's death, the emphasis here is upon Christ as the Priest who made the sacrifice of Himself. In addition, the book reveals an area of Christ's ministry untouched in other volumes: His present priestly ministry of intercession. Paul mentioned that Christ was at the right hand of God, making intercession for believers (Rom. 8:34); the Book of Hebrews describes the nature of that intercession: "But this man, because he continueth ever, hath an unchangeable priesthood. Wherefore he is able also to save them to the uttermost that come unto God by him, seeing he ever liveth to make intercession for them" (7:24-25).

The key passage on the exposition of divine chastisement is also found here (12:3-12). A believer should not despise the chastening of God, but he should endure it and profit spiritually from it. Chastisement is a sign of divine love and sonship; lack of it may indicate an illegitimate relationship or an unregenerate heart. It should produce reverence, submission, peace, righteousness, and encouragement in the believer's life.

The Book of Hebrews also contains the "Faith Hall of Fame" (11:1-40). The Old Testament characters of Abel, Enoch, Noah, Abraham, Isaac, Jacob, Joseph, Moses, Joshua, Rahab, and others are cited as examples of men and women who believed that "[God] is, and that he is a rewarder of them that diligently seek him" (11:6). These endured the persecutions of the world because they trusted God. The famous definition of faith is set forth here: "Now faith is the substance of things hoped for, the evidence of things not seen" (11:1). Whenever evangelical Christians think of the subject of faith, their minds automatically turn to Hebrews 11.

The book is full of warnings, inserted at various intervals within the presentation of the author's theme (2:1-4; 3:7-9; 4:1-13; 5:11—6:20; 10:26-31; 12:14-17; 12:18-29). The writer did not want to wait until his conclusion to apply the truths to the lives of his readers. These warnings were signaled by the sevenfold use of "lest" (2:1; 3:12, 13; 4:11; 12:3, 13, 15).

The author involved himself in the commands he directed toward his readers by making use of the Greek hortatory subjunctive. These are all introduced by the words "Let us. . . ." Here is a listing of the thirteen instances:

1. "Let us therefore fear" (4:1).
2. "Let us labour therefore to enter into that rest" (4:11).
3. "Let us hold fast our profession" (4:14).
4. "Let us therefore come boldly unto the throne of grace" (4:16).
5. "Let us go on unto perfection" (6:1).
6. "Let us draw near with a true heart in full assurance of faith" (10:22).
7. "Let us hold fast the profession of our faith without wavering" (10:23).
8. "Let us consider one another to provoke unto love and to good works" (10:24).
9. "Let us lay aside every weight" (12:1).
10. "Let us run with patience the race that is set before us" (12:1).
11. "Let us have grace" (12:28).
12. "Let us go forth therefore unto him without the camp" (13:13).
13. "Let us offer the sacrifice of praise to God continually" (13:15).

This type of command was not as direct or harsh as a regular imperative.[5] The author thus spoke to himself as well as to his readers.

The key word of the book is "better." The word is used thirteen times to show the superiority of the believer's position in Christ (1:4; 6:9; 7:7, 19, 22; 8:6 [twice]; 9:23; 10:34; 11:16, 35, 40). In Christ the believer has better promises and a better hope, covenant, substance, country, and resurrection.

5. Compare "Let us fear" with "Fear ye." The second is more direct.

Prophets, Angels, and the Son
Hebrews 1:1–14

The book begins as other key biblical books do—with God (Gen. 1:1; John 1:1; I John 1:1). The author definitely accepts the divine origin and authority for the inscripturated revelation of both Testaments.

He regards his work as a brief letter, specifically as a "word of exhortation" (13:22). In synagogue services exhortations usually followed the reading of the Law and the Prophets (Acts 13:15). Most commentators believe that the book "begins like a treatise, continues like a sermon, and ends like a letter."[1] Hughes states that the Book of Hebrews is "the most extensively developed and logically sustained piece of theological argumentation in the whole of the New Testament."[2] The doctrinal thesis of the superiority of the divine revelation in Jesus Christ is presented in the first ten chapters (1:1—10:18), followed by practical admonitions (10:19—13:25).

I. BETTER THAN THE PROPHETS (1:1–3)

In the opening three verses contrasts are made between the revelation given in the Old Testament prophets and that which was seen in Jesus Christ. They involve time, recipients, method,

1. A. T. Robertson, *Word Pictures in the New Testament* (Nashville: Broadman, 1932), V:328.
2. P. E. Hughes, *A Commentary on the Epistle to the Hebrews* (Grand Rapids: Eerdmans, 1977), p. 35.

and agency. In the midst of these differences, however, there is a strong continuity of progressive revelation, because God is the one who has chosen to speak through both channels. The two verbs ("spake" and "hath spoken") show this movement from the old to the new.[3]

A. Revelation in the Prophets (1:1)

The opening verse contains five assertions about the nature of prophetic revelation.

1. Divine communication

"God . . . spake . . . by the prophets." The source of authority is God, not man. The emphasis is on the declaration that *God* spoke, and the sphere of that speaking is literally "in" (*en*) the prophets. God was in the prophets at the time they wrote and proclaimed authoritative truth to their audiences. Prophecy did not originate within the thought processes or willful desires of the sages; rather, these "holy men of God spake as they were moved by the Holy Ghost" (II Peter 1:21). What they wrote and spoke was literally inspired, or breathed out, by God (II Tim. 3:16).

Peter claimed that the spirit of Christ was *in* the prophets at the time they testified (I Peter 1:11). Throughout Scripture there is a natural equation of God and man in the production of Holy Writ. Often the seers began their oracular pronouncements with the introductory formula: "And the word of the Lord came unto me, saying" (cf. Zech. 6:9). Godly men, like Zacharias the priest, acknowledged that the God of Israel spoke "by the mouth of his holy prophets" (Luke 1:70). The apostles charged that the Holy Spirit spoke by the writers of the Old Testament books (Acts 1:16; 28:25). What was spoken by God could be seen in what was written by the divinely authenticated spokesmen (Deut. 18:15–22).

There is also an obvious contrast between the plural prophets

---

3. Both verbs are in the aorist tense and are built upon the stem *laleō*.

and the singular Son. These prophets include not only the writing prophets (e.g., Isaiah), but also the speaking prophets who did not author any of the biblical books (e.g., Elijah). They also embrace those who had both the prophetic gift and office (e.g., Zechariah), and those who had only the gift (e.g., David).

The prophets were not passive. As men burdened over the moral and doctrinal sins of their people, they cried out for repentance. In so doing they became the voice of God to Israel. The rejection of the prophetic message was, in essence, the repudiation of God Himself.

2. At different times

The phrase "at sundry times" literally means "many portions" (polumerōs).[4] God did not reveal all of His mind or will at one given time in the Old Testament period; rather, He progressively revealed truth at different times through His official spokesmen. In fact, it took about one thousand years to produce the authoritative canon of Israel from the ministry of Moses to that of Malachi (1400–400 B.C.). This span of time is known as the "other ages" (Eph. 3:5).

Each prophetic announcement built upon preceding declarations and prepared the way for future, unborn spokesmen. The gradual revelation of divine truth followed this pattern: "For precept must be upon precept, precept upon precept; line upon line, line upon line; here a little, and there a little" (Isa. 28:10). Paul claimed that prophecy was always partial (I Cor. 13:9).

3. In different ways

The phrase "in divers manners" (polutropōs)[5] points to the various modes of divine revelation in the ages before Christ. God manifested Himself and His word in unusual ways then. He appeared as the visible angel of the Lord to Abraham (Gen. 22:15). He spoke to Moses out of a burning bush (Exod. 3:2–4). On Mount Sinai He inscribed the Ten Commandments on two

---

4. Used only here in the New Testament.
5. Used only here in the New Testament.

tablets of stone with His own hand (Exod. 32:16). He spoke to Elijah in a "still small voice" (I Kings 19:12). Daniel received dreams and visions (Dan. 7:1). In addition, there were angelic visitations and multiple theophanies.

There was no set pattern to the mode of divine revelation. God initiated the communication, and in many cases, the prophets were personally surprised by the abruptness and uniqueness of the events.

4. In time past

The phrase "in time past" (*palai*) must be seen in contrast to "the last days" in which God revealed Himself in His Son. Christ described this period thusly: "For all the prophets and the law prophesied until John" (Matt. 11:13). John the Baptist was the last of the Old Testament prophets. His ministry terminated the revelatory age of the past, although the written expression of divine revelation ended with the Book of Malachi.

5. To the fathers

This phrase technically refers to the entire nation of Old Testament Israel. Paul made this equation (Rom. 9:5). Christ used the phrase to identify that generation of Israelites who lived during the ministry of Moses (John 6:58; 7:22). Although Abraham, Isaac, and Jacob are described as the patriarchs of the Hebrew people, the usage of the phrase in this verse definitely goes beyond their lifetimes and the historical scope of Genesis.

B. Revelation in the Son (1:2-3)

Attention is now shifted to Jesus Christ. Eight statements are given to demonstrate His superiority to the prophets.

1. He is the climax of revelation

God spoke literally "in Son" (*en huiōi*). No definite article ("the") is used before the noun. This grammatical feature stresses the quality or nature of His sonship. Stress is not only on what Christ said and did, but especially on what and who He is. The prophets spoke the word of God, but Christ *is* the word of God (John 1:1). He did not become the Son because God spoke in Him; rather, He was always the eternal Son of God. The divine revelation, communicated in and through Him, became visible, human, and personal at His incarnation and His subsequent earthly ministry. John declared, "No man hath seen God at any time; the only begotten Son, which is in the bosom of the Father, he hath declared him" (John 1:18).

The qualifying phrase "in these last days" is set in contrast to the "time past" of the prophetic era. It points to the climax of divine authoritative revelation. Although the apostles and their approved associates produced the New Testament books after the earthly ministry of Christ, they actually only expounded the significance of His death and resurrection by the superintendence of the Holy Spirit. Christ anticipated the canon when He predicted that the Spirit would remind the apostles, teach them, and guide them into prophetic truth (John 14:26; 16:13). The Savior clearly enunciated the purpose of the Spirit's advent: "He shall glorify me: for he shall receive of mine, and shall shew it unto you" (John 16:14). The distinction in the Book of Hebrews is always between the speaking of the Old Testament prophets and that of Christ, never of the apostles (2:2-4; 12:25).

The recipients ("unto us") of the new revelation embrace both the writer of the book and his readers. Both constitute a representative group for the entire church, the family of God that Christ is building in this age (Matt. 16:18).

2. He is the heir

These two verses now contain three relative pronouns ("whom," "whom," and "who") which present a series of seven statements that show the superiority of the Son.

As the sovereign Creator, God naturally owns all things (I Cor.

10:26). He made the universe; therefore, it belongs to Him. As the eternal Son of God, co-equal with the Father and the Spirit in the Trinitarian oneness of the divine Being, Christ also has dominion over all.

The appointment to heirship, however, does not refer to that eternal prerogative of deity. It rather points to that feature of the eternal decree in which the Father appointed the Son to be the heir as the result of the Son's willingness to be the revealer of God and the Redeemer of lost mankind (John 1:1, 14, 18). The humiliation and condescension of the Son, which led to His incarnation through the virgin conception and His substitution-ary death on the cross, later eventuated in His triumphant resurrection and His ascension into an exalted position in the heavens (Phil. 2:6-11). In the Great Commission Christ declared to the apostles that all power had been given to Him in heaven and in earth (Matt. 28:18).

Dominion over the planet Earth was given to Adam, but he lost that control through his sin (2:5-8). The eternal Son of God became man in order to regain that dominion for man. He earned that right through His redemptive work, but He has not yet claimed the title deed to the universe, the seven-sealed scroll seen in the Father's hand (Rev. 5:1-7). The psalmist records this offer of the Father to the Son:

> I will declare the decree: the LORD hath said unto me, Thou art my Son, this day have I begotten thee.
>
> Ask of me, and I shall give thee the heathen for thine inheritance, and the uttermost parts of the earth for thy possession (Ps. 2:7-8).

Christ has not yet asked for what is rightfully His. He will not do so until the onset of the Great Tribulation period.

The divine appointment is certain, but its appropriation by Christ is still future. Believers, as regenerated spiritual children and adopted sons of God, also enjoy the position of heirship with Christ (Rom. 8:17; Gal. 4:7).

3. He made the ages

The Father, through the Son ("by whom"), made the time-space universe. The word "worlds" (*aiōnas*) is better translated as "ages." It deals with time and the movement of history from one generation to another. God is in sovereign control over the affairs of men and nations. Paul declared on Mars Hill to the Athenian philosophers that God "hath made of one blood all nations of men for to dwell on all of the face of the earth, and hath determined the times before appointed, and the bounds of their habitation" (Acts 17:26). Daniel testified that God "changeth the times and the seasons: he removeth kings, and setteth up kings" (Dan. 2:21).

The entire triune Godhead shared in the creation of the material and immaterial world (Gen. 1:1; John 1:1-3; I Cor. 8:6). So it is with the framing of human destiny. Some have identified history as "His story." That simple phrase is more profound than it seems. Unless the daily affairs of humanity are related to their divine agent of guidance, they lose their eternal meaning and significance. Ever since the creation of man, the goal of history has been the establishment of the kingdom of God on earth with Christ as its divine-human monarch.

4. He has divine glory

The next declaration has two possible interpretations that are accepted as viable evangelical options.

The first view, held by such men as Calvin and Thayer, contends that Christ manifested the brightness of divine glory in the perfection of His manhood through which He revealed God and redeemed man. It therefore was a reflected brightness, or a refulgence. Just as Moses reflected the glory of God in the brightness of his countenance after being in the presence of God for forty days on Mount Sinai (II Cor. 3:7), so Christ perfectly reflected the glory of the Father in that He was always in the fellowship of the Father. The relationship of reflection, consequently, is likened to that of the moon to the sun. This position does not deny the eternal ontological glory of God the Son; rather, it emphasizes the postincarnation life of the Savior.

The second view seems to be held by the majority of evangelical writers.[6] It states that Christ manifested in His human existence that eternal glory which was innately His as one of the Persons of the Trinitarian, monotheistic, divine Being. The brightness therefore was a radiation of holiness as from an original light source. He thus would be compared to the sun.

The term "brightness" (*apaugasma*)[7] comes from a verb which can mean either "radiate" or "reflect." The sense of radiation denotes an effulgence of glory.

The "glory" is the full manifestation of the divine attributes and essence. Christ had that glory even before the world existed (John 17:5). Isaiah saw that preincarnate glory (Isa. 6:1–8; John 12:41). Men viewed that glorious expression of grace and truth in His earthly ministry (John 1:14). It is true that Christ prayed for a restoration of His eternal glory (John 17:5). This restoration occurred after His death and resurrection, but it simply meant that He was subsequently seen in an outward demonstration of His glorious self whereas that expression was previously veiled within human flesh. On the Mount of Transfiguration, the three apostles saw Christ's deity displayed as the glory of His divine person shone right through His natural body (Matt. 17:1–13; II Peter 1:16–18).

The participle "being" (*ōn*)[8] further points out Christ's absolute, timeless existence. The phrase thus is comparable to "being in the form of God" (Phil. 2:6). The Son of God is all that God the Father is. They are one (John 10:30).

5. He is the image of God

Christ is also "the express image of his person." The term "express image" (*charaktēr*)[9] indicates that He is the perfect representation of the divine essence. The English word "character" is an obvious transliteration of the Greek term. The term originally referred to the engraving tool, then to the die made

6. Included among them are Hughes, *A Commentary on . . . Hebrews,* p. 42, and Thomas Hewitt, *The Epistle to the Hebrews,* (Grand Rapids: Eerdmans, 1981), p. 52.

7. Used only here in the New Testament.

8. Present participle of *eimi.*

9. Used only here in the New Testament.

by the tool, and finally to the mark made upon a coin by the die.

Since God is an omnipresent spirit being, no man has the ability to see Him (John 1:18). God the Son, therefore, took to Himself a perfect, complete human nature in order to reveal God to man. If a person wants to see God, then he has only to look at Jesus Christ. This is the very reason why He boldly asserted: ". . .he that hath seen me hath seen the Father" (John 14:9). This intrapersonal oneness was further elucidated in His declaration: "Believe me that I am in the Father, and the Father in me" (John 14:11).

The term "person" (*hupostaseōs*) literally means "that which stands under." It refers to the foundation underneath a building. In this passage it refers to the divine nature or essence that is fundamental to the being of God. Elsewhere it is used of "faith" as "the substance of things hoped for" (Heb. 11:1). It is also translated as "confidence" (3:14; II Cor. 9:4; 11:17).

6. He is the Governor

Christ has the ministry of "upholding all things by the word of his power." He has a providential purpose for the universe. The participle "upholding" (*pherōn*) implies not only support, but also direction or movement toward a goal. Christ created the time–space universe, and He also sustains it (Col. 1:17). In addition, He is achieving His predetermined purpose for man-kind as He guides the ages toward the elimination of His enemies and the establishment of the eternal state of righteous-ness (I Cor. 15:24–25). He will bring things and persons to their proper end. There will be no temporal loss of that which has eternal significance to Him.

The means of this accomplishment is God's Word. He will do what He says because He has the power to execute His will. All men should acknowledge that "he doeth according to his will in the army of heaven, and among the inhabitants of the earth: and none can stay his hand, or say unto him, What doest thou?" (Dan. 4:35). God is the sovereign governor of the affairs of nations. He can work in and through the actions of both good and evil men to accomplish the ultimate purpose of His glorification. In so doing, God will hold men accountable for their evil deeds and will reward the righteous for their works of goodness.

7. He is the Redeemer

Four aspects of Christ's redemptive work are enumerated here. First, it was an exclusive work. He did it "by Himself." There was no other who could die for mankind. He was the Kinsman Redeemer. He alone satisfied the righteous demands of God for sin. Salvation thus is in Him and in what He did. No man can become a co-redeemer with Christ by the addition of his own effort to the gracious death of the Savior.

Second, Christ achieved a sacrificial work of cleansing. The verb "had purged" literally means "having made a purification" (*katharismon poiēsamenos*). The English term "catharsis" is based upon this Greek noun. It is used elsewhere for an animal sacrifice of cleansing (Mark 1:44). Its adjectival form is translated usually as "pure" (Matt. 5:8) or "clean" (John 13:10; 15:3). His sacrifice therefore was designed to produce a thorough moral cleansing.

Third, Christ finished this task in His own interest. The aorist tense of the participle ("having made") shows that He completed His redemptive work once and for all. When Christ died He triumphantly exclaimed: "It is finished" (John 19:30). The middle voice of the verbal form reveals the fact that Christ had a self-interest in what He did. Men, of course, benefit from the cross, but the greatest result of the cross was Christ's own glorification.

Fourth, Christ cleansed men from their sins. This action includes their practice, pollution, and penalty.

8. He is seated in heaven

In the tabernacle constructed by Moses in the wilderness or in the temple built by Solomon there were no chairs on which the priests could sit. The absence of seats indicated that their work was never completed and that men could not sit in the presence of the holy God of Israel. Christ, however, "sat down" after He offered the priestly sacrifice of Himself. This action of seating demonstrated the finality of His redemptive work, the historical verification of His resurrection and ascension, His exalted position as head of the church (Eph. 1:20-23), and His equality with the Father. This official seating fulfilled the promise of the Father to the Son: "Sit thou at my right hand, until I make thine enemies thy footstool" (Ps. 110:1).

II. BETTER THAN THE ANGELS (1:4-14)

In the Old Testament era, God sometimes spoke by angels (2:2). Angels had a part in the giving of the law to Moses (Acts 7:53; Gal. 3:19). The author therefore had to demonstrate the superiority of Christ to the angels as the Mediator and Redeemer.

The Dead Sea Scrolls have indicated that the Qumran sect believed in the advent of two messiahs, that the kingly messiah would be subordinate to the priestly messiah, that both messiahs would be under Michael the archangel, and that angels would be over men in the kingdom. Some evangelical writers suggest that the writing of the Book of Hebrews must be seen against that religious, cultural background of the first century.

A. Statement of Superiority (1:4)

1. He became better

In His deity, God the Son is naturally better than the angels; however, He also became better in His humanity. The participle "being made" (*genomenos*) can also mean "having come to be." It is the same verb used of His incarnation (John 1:14). The verb used of His eternal deity is different than this one (cf. *ōn*; 1:3; John 1:1).

In the order of creation, man is lower than the angels (2:7).

By becoming human, Christ condescended to a position lower than the angels, but He has been exalted through His death, resurrection, and ascension to a position higher than them.

2. He has inherited a better name

God gave to Christ "a name which is above every name" (Phil. 2:9). All will bow before Christ to acknowledge His lordship over the eternal kingdom. His appointment as heir of all things secured for Him this "more excellent name." He obtained the exalted name through His perfect obedience to the redemptive will of God. Only in His name can salvation be appropriated (Acts 4:12).

B. Proof of Superiority (1:5–14)

The remaining part of this chapter contains a series of seven quotations from the Old Testament. They are designed to prove that Christ, in both His deity and humanity, is superior to the angels.

1. His begetting (1:5a)

Angels collectively are known as the "sons of God" (Job 1:6), but no angel has ever been individually addressed by God as His son. Sinful men can become children of God through divine regeneration and sons of God by divine adoption.

This quotation from a Davidic, messianic psalm (Ps. 2:7), however, demonstrates the uniqueness of Christ's sonship. His sonship was declared in the birth announcement to Mary (Luke 1:32), at His baptism (Mark 1:11), at His transfiguration (Luke 9:35), and through His resurrection (Rom. 1:4).

In what sense, though, did the Father beget the Son? Three major views have emerged within evangelicalism. The first looks at this declaration as a proof of the eternal generation of the Son. The Nicene Creed (A.D. 325) states that Christ is "the only-begotten Son of God, begotten of the Father before all

31

worlds; Light of Light, very God of very God, begotten not made." In that choice of words, the early church fathers wanted to point out the unique eternal relationship between the Father and the Son without implying that the Son had a beginning in time. There could be no Father without the Son and there could be no Son without the Father. The decree, therefore, is as eternal as the relationship.

The second view relates the begetting to the resurrection of Christ.[10] There is some evidence that Paul used this same quotation in a synagogue sermon to prove that the Messiah had to die and to rise again (Acts 13:33-38).

The third view sees the fulfillment of the quotation in the incarnation of the Son through the virgin conception.[11] The same verb "begotten" (*gennaō*) is used in Gabriel's announcement to Mary: ". . .that holy thing which shall be [begotten] of thee shall be called the Son of God" (Luke 1:35). Only the eternal Son of God could become the Messiah of Israel, the seed of the woman, who would destroy Satan (Gen. 3:15). The begetting thus refers to the introduction of the human existence of the Son.

2. His royal relation (1:5b)

The second quotation comes from the midst of the Davidic covenant (II Sam. 7:14). God promised that the house, throne, and kingdom of David would be established forever (II Sam. 7:4-17). Although there was a reference to Solomon as the son of David and the heir of the promises, the greater fulfillment was to be in the Jewish Messiah, the true son of David. The religious teachers of Israel in the first century firmly believed that the Messiah would be the son of David (Matt. 22:41-42). The followers of Christ thus constantly affirmed Him to be the son of David (Matt. 1:1; 9:27; Rom. 1:3).

10. Hughes, A Commentary on . . . Hebrews, p. 54.
11. Held by John R. Rice, *Is Jesus God?* (Grand Rapids: Zondervan, 1948), p. 71; and John F. Walvoord, *Jesus Christ Our Lord* (Chicago: Moody, 1969), p. 40. Author's view also. For more discussion, see the author's book *The Virgin Birth: Doctrine of Deity* (Grand Rapids: Baker, 1981), chap. 5.

No angel could ever be the messianic king of Israel, the ruler of planet Earth. This dominion, thus, is based upon His incarnation and His birth into the royal family. He must be the Son of David, the son of Abraham, and the son of Adam.

3. His worship (1:6)

The position of the adverb ("again") is critical to the interpretation of this next declaration. It could refer to just another quotation in the series.[12] In the Greek text, however, it may modify the verb in the temporal clause: "And whenever he again brings. . . ."[13] This second possibility looks at Christ's second coming to earth to reign as King rather than to His incarnation.

The title "firstborn" (*prōtotokon*) is messianic. God said of Jesus: "Also I will make him my firstborn, higher than the kings of the earth" (Ps. 89:27). Paul ascribed this title to Christ because of the latter's incarnation and resurrection (Rom. 8:29; Col. 1:15, 18). The term connotes priority and superiority.

The worship of Christ by the angels, mentioned in the quotation (Deut. 32:43 in the Septuagint Greek text), did occur at His birth in Bethlehem (Luke 2:13); however, they will accompany Christ at His second advent and will worship Him then also (Matt. 24:30; 25:31). Since it is wrong for any creature to worship another creature, the worship of Christ by the angels, commanded by the Father, is another indication of His deity.

4. His ministers (1:7)

Angels are created "spirits" (*pneumata*). They serve as God's "ministers" (*leitourgous*). The English term "liturgy" is based upon this Greek word. Their ministry always reveals their religious devotion. In such service they may use the winds (another translation of *pneumata*) and fire as the channels for their manifestation. This physical expression is in stark contrast to the permanent acquisition of a human nature by the Son.

12. KJV, NIV, RSV.
13. ASV. The text reads, "*hotan de palin eisagagēi.* . . ."

The temporary nature of wind and fire shows also the transitory ministry of angels in contrast to the permanent work of the Savior. This Old Testament quotation (Ps. 104:4) also points out that angels have been created to serve the Son.

5. His royal deity (1:8–9)

Five concepts can be seen in this fifth quotation (Ps. 45:6–7). First, God the Father addressed the Son as "O God." One person of the Trinitarian God is ascribing deity to another divine person. The noun ("O God") must thus be seen as a vocative of direct address. Some, however, translate this phrase thusly: "God is thy throne."[14] In His earthly ministry Christ did identify God as His God (John 20:17). In support of the first reading, however, Thomas addressed Christ as his God (John 20:28). Israel knew that its Messiah would be known as "the mighty God" (Isa. 9:6). Christ argued that He was divine as well as Davidic (Matt. 22:41–46).

Second, Christ is destined to have an eternal throne and kingdom.

Third, His reign will be righteous (1:8b). This is the quality of the messianic kingdom (Isa. 11:3-5).

Fourth, He "loved righteousness and hated iniquity" during His earthly sojourn. In the expression of His humanity, He totally pleased the Father. He was the acme of holiness.

Fifth, God rewarded the obedience of the Son with an exaltation above all men. The term "fellows" (metochous) is based upon the same verb used of Christ when He "took part" (metesche; 2:14) of the nature of man.

6. His permanence (1:10–12)

This extensive quotation (Ps. 102:25–27) contains three aspects of Christ's deity. First, He created the earth and the heavens (1:10). He brought them into existence out of nothing

---

14. Robertson allows this possibility. *Word Pictures,* p. 339. It is accepted by Wycliffe, Tyndale, Moffatt, Westcott, and Goodspeed. It is found in the marginal notations of the RSV and NEB.

by His divine will and skill. The created universe displays His power and wisdom.

Second, He will sovereignly take the created order out of existence (1:11–12a). The present universe is temporary, not eternal. It had a beginning, and it will have an ending. It will "perish" and it will "wax old." The earth is not only aging, but it is also becoming polluted. Its resources are being used up. But man will not terminate this universe; Christ will. He will "fold up" the earth and heavens as useless garments. He will burn up this universe by fire in order to create a new heaven and earth (Matt. 24:35; II Peter 3:7; Rev. 21:1).

Third, Christ is immutable (Mal. 3:6). He is "the same yesterday, and today, and forever" (13:8). He "remains" (1:11a). He is eternally constant. His deity is not diminished by the passing of time, and He will never surrender His humanity throughout eternity.

7. *His position (1:13–14)*

Christ used this quotation (Ps. 110:1) to argue that the Messiah had to be divine as well as human (Matt. 22:41–46).

The Father invited the Son to sit in the heavenly presence after Christ's crucifixion, resurrection, and ascension (1:3). In the conclusion of the letter to the Laodicean church, Christ stated: ". . .even as I also overcame, and am set down with my Father in his throne" (Rev. 3:21). Christ will remain there until He comes to earth to destroy His enemies at Armageddon.

Until the Second Advent occurs, angels are sent forth as heavenly apostles to minister to those men who will enjoy the benefits of Christ's accomplished salvation throughout eternity. The popular notion of "guardian angels" is somewhat based upon this concept. There is no indication in Scripture what the exact ministry of an angel to a believer is.

Questions for Discussion

1. Does God speak to men today in dreams? In visions? Defend your answer.

2. Why do some believe that the words of Jesus are more authoritative than the statements of Paul? Is there any difference between authority and importance?

3. Some people have claimed to have seen Christ in the heavens. Did they really? If not, what or whom did they see?

4. What arguments are used by the cults to reject the deity of Christ? How can they be refuted?

5. How does the ministry of Christ relate to the convictions of contemporary science, history, and sociology?

6. What is involved in biblical worship? What can men learn about worship from the angels?

7. In what ways could angels minister to men today? Could a UFO be an angelic visitation?

The Exaltation of Man
Hebrews 2:1-18

The relationship of Jesus Christ to the angels continues in this chapter. His superiority to the heavenly messengers is seen in three major areas: His deity, His humanity, and His redemptive work. This demonstration is necessary in order to set up the contrast between the word spoken by angels and that spoken by Christ (2:2-3).

In the first two chapters, angels are mentioned eleven times (1:4, 5, 6, 7 [twice], 13; 2:2, 5, 7, 9, 16). The noun appears twice elsewhere in the epistle (12:22; 13:2). Since angels are only enumerated fourteen times in all of the Pauline epistles, their emphasis in Hebrews becomes even more remarkable.

I. THE FIRST WARNING (2:1-4)

Seven warnings are inserted at key intervals throughout the book (2:1-4; 3:7-13; 4:1-13; 5:11—6:20; 10:26-31; 12:14-17; 12:18-39). They are designed to produce encouragement, obedience, maturity, perseverance, and faith. They contain threats of chastisement, discipline, and loss of spiritual privilege.

The conjunction "therefore" bases this appeal on what has already been stated (1:4-14). The warning then gives rise to a further discussion of the superiority of Christ to the angels (2:5-18).

37

A. Its Nature (2:1)

1. Positive

The warning has both a positive and a negative feature. The verb "ought" (*dei*) points out the moral and logical necessity for compliance to revealed truth. For the child of God, obedience is commanded, not requested. The author includes himself with his readers as those who must practice truth ("we").

To "give heed" (*prosechein*) means "to attach oneself to, to adhere to, to give assent to." It involves an active, constant commitment to a cause or a conviction.[1] The urgency to do so is intensified by the addition of the adverb ("more earnest"). The appeal is for spiritual alertness, comprehension of moral consequences, and an internal compulsion to be totally obedient.

The body of doctrinal truth is identified as "the things which we have heard."[2] It is later described as "so great salvation" (2:3). This redemptive gospel, centered in the death and resurrection of Christ, was spoken originally by the Savior during His earthly ministry, was heard directly by the apostles, and was received subsequently by the author and his readers. Elsewhere this redemptive core is called "the doctrine of Christ" (II John 9), "the faith" (I Tim. 4:1), and "the faith which was once delivered unto the saints" (Jude 3).

2. Negative

The negative particle "lest" (*mē*) introduces the alternative to obedience. The adverb ("at any time," *pote*) indicates that even one act of deliberate rebellion is too much. In real life, some sins and errors of judgment produce irreversible results of tragedy.[3] Some acts of moral disobedience, therefore, leave no time for repentance and recovery.

1. The verb form is a present active infinitive.
2. Literally, "the things which have been heard" (*tois akoustheisi:* aorist passive participle).
3. For example, jumping out of an airplane without a parachute or with a faulty chute.

The verbal action literally translates: "lest we should slip away" (*pararruōmen*).[4] Accountability thus rests with each believer. The verb is used of a river flowing by and of a boat gliding by or drifting away. In the analogy, a dock or a point of anchor can be equated with the revealed, heard truth of Christ, whereas the believer is likened to a boat. He faces the moral consequences for a willful refusal to attach himself to doctrinal and spiritual obedience. The believer, thus, will be tested in his relationship to the superior revelation.

B. Its Reason (2:2-4)

The reason for the warning is introduced by the explanatory conjunction ("for"). It contains an argument from the lesser to the greater, from the angelic word to the proclamations of Christ and the apostles. It includes three aspects of the spoken word.

1. Word of the angels (2:2)

Four features of angelic participation in divine revelation can be seen. First, the "word spoken by angels" refers to both the direct, vocal pronouncements (Gen. 19:1-15) and the giving of the Mosaic Law (Deut. 33:1-2; Ps. 68:17). Stephen declared that the law was given "by the disposition of angels" (Acts 7:53). Paul claimed that the law "was ordained by angels in the hand of a mediator" (Gal. 3:19). Although the Old Testament historical account of the giving of the law on Sinai contains no mention of the angels, they were involved.

Second, the angels' word was "stedfast." It was sure and firm. It was valid and binding on all parties. It could not be challenged.

Third, the angels' word could be violated in two ways. The concept behind "transgression" is a violation of a negative commandment: "Thou shalt not. . . ." It is doing what the law prohibited. The term (*parabasis*) literally means "to go beyond."

4. Present active subjunctive.

The sense behind "disobedience" is a violation of a positive commandment: "Thou shalt. . . ." It is not doing what the law commanded. Its Greek term (*parakoē*) literally means "to hear beside." Both sins, of course, issued from willful rebellion, not from an ignorance of the law.

Fourth, violators of their word were judged. Sinners received "a just recompense of reward." The nature of the punishment was explicitly described within the law. Men knew what they would get if they chose to break the law. In some cases, restitution and penalties had to be made, and in others, capital punishment followed. The law matched the penalty to the crime. It exacted justice; it offered no mercy.

2. Word of Christ (2:3a)

The conclusion of the conditional clause is now given in the form of a question, started by the interrogative pronoun ("how").[5] The basic question is very simple: "How shall we escape. . .?" The author again includes himself with his readers ("we"). No direct object for the verb is stated, but it is implied from the preceding verse. No contemporary believer can escape his just recompense of reward if he transgresses or disobeys what Christ has said. The violation of divine revelation through angels brought judgment to the offenders; consequently, the violation of divine revelation through a superior mediator, namely Christ, will likewise bring the same response.

The essence of "neglect" (*amelēsantes*) literally means "no care or concern."[6] Elsewhere the verb is used of those men who "made light" of the invitation to the marriage feast (Matt. 22:5). Paul warned Timothy not to neglect his spiritual gift (I Tim. 4:14). Peter did not want to "be negligent" in reminding his congregation about eschatological truth (II Peter 1:12). Apathy and indifference mark this type of disobedience.

The word of Christ is described as "so great salvation." It is great because God designed it to His own glory (Eph. 1:3-14),

5. A first class conditional Greek clause can be seen in verse 2, started by "if" (*ei*).
6. The KJV regards the aorist form as a conditional participle.

because it took the incarnation, crucifixion, and resurrection of God the Son to make it available, and because it makes saints out of sinners.

During His earthly ministry, Christ referred to His death and resurrection in disguised metaphors to His critics: the sign of Jonah in the fish for three days and nights (Matt. 12:38-40) and the destruction and rebuilding of the temple in three days (John 2:18-22). After Christ announced His new program for the church, He explicitly declared His coming passion to the disciples (Matt. 16:21; 17:22-23; 20:17-19; 26:2, 31-32). He spoke of Himself as the Good Shepherd who would sacrifice His life for the sheep (John 10:11) and as the grain of wheat which had to die in the ground in order to bear fruit (John 12:24). After His resurrection, He again proclaimed the divine purpose for His death and commanded the apostles to preach this new gospel (Luke 24:46-49).

3. Word of the apostles (2:3b–4)

The apostles are identified as "them that heard him." Christ originally selected twelve men from among His followers to become His apostles. They were to be with Him; then He would send them forth to preach, to heal, and to cast out demons (Matt. 10:1). Their outreach was limited to Israel at the first and their message centered in the imminence of the kingdom (Matt. 10:5-8). After His resurrection, Christ recommissioned the Eleven to proclaim the gospel of His redemptive work to all men (Matt. 28:16-20). Apostles, then, were men who saw the resurrected Christ and who were commanded directly by Him to preach. Paul claimed that he received his apostolic authority in this fashion (I Cor. 9:1; 15:8-11; Gal. 1:1). Few men in the New Testament era possessed this leadership position.

God authenticated or confirmed these official spokesmen with abilities that other believers did not have. Four aspects of this confirmation are listed here. First, the meaning of confirmation is the guarantee or authentication of God that an apostolic ministry is genuine. The verb (*ebebaiōthē*) is used in the early

Greek papyri for the legal sense of guarantee. Christ confirmed the word of the apostles by the signs that followed (Mark 16:20). Paul claimed that his pioneer ministry in Corinth was confirmed (I Cor. 1:6). He later admitted that he possessed the signs of an apostle (II Cor. 12:12). In the early church the apostles and their official representatives performed the miracles (Acts 2:43; 3:6; 5:12).

Second, the recipients of the confirmation were those who heard the apostles ("unto us"). The apostles knew that they were apostles, but others needed to be convinced that the former were official spokesmen for God. God established this principle when He gave to Israel the data by which they could determine who was a true or a false prophet (Deut. 18:20–22). Paul reported that his miraculous deeds were wrought among the Corinthians (I Cor. 1:6; II Cor. 12:12). In addition, the converts of the apostles were then enabled to exercise revelatory and authenticating gifts (I Cor. 1:7).

Third, the companion of confirmation was God ("God also bearing witness"). The apostles spoke, but God spoke through them and enabled the word to produce fruit in the listeners. Paul asserted that his proclamation was "in demonstration of the Spirit and of power" (I Cor. 2:4).

Fourth, the nature of confirmation was fourfold. *Signs* are miracles which reveal divine purpose, bear witness to the truth of the proclamation, and manifest spiritual significance. The *what* of the miracle becomes overshadowed by the *why* of the event. *Wonders* show the uniqueness of the miracle. They attract attention and promote awe and amazement. These spectacular phenomena call attention to supernatural workings which could not be duplicated by man. *Divers miracles* refer to the demonstration of divine power in all realms: cleansing leprosy, raising the dead, restoring sight and speech, and healing those with palsy. These three words are used together to show the divine approval of the ministries of Christ (Acts 2:22) and of Paul (II Cor. 12:12).[7] *The gifts of the Holy Spirit* refer to those special abilities given to a first-century believer through the apostles by the Spirit (I Cor. 12:4–11).

7. They are *sēmeion* (sign), *tera* (wonder), and *dunamis* (power).

The divine authentication is according to God's own will (cf. I Cor. 12:7, 11).

II. THE RESTORATION OF MAN (2:5-18)

The argument of the superiority of Christ to the angels continues in this section. It is based upon the sovereignty promised to mankind in Adam (Gen. 1:26-27), but lost through the fall of man by sin. Christ, however, as the perfect man, has regained for man that lost dominion through His redemptive work. Rulership over the earth was never offered to the angels, thus Christ has exalted man to a position even higher than the angels.

A. The Significance of Man (2:5-8)

1. His rulership (2:5)

This fact is implied in the lack of dominion given to the angels. No angel or group of angels could expect to rule over the planet either in this age or in the one to come. The term "world" (*oikoumenēn*) refers to the inhabited earth of mankind (Matt. 24:14; Luke 2:1; 4:5). It literally means "to remain in the house." The earth is the house in which man abides today.

The dominion mentioned in this verse, however, points to the world "to come." Literally, it is "the one which is about to be" (*tēn mellousan*). It refers to the millennial kingdom, the theocratic monarchy promised in the Davidic covenant (II Sam. 7:16) and to its extension into the new heavens and the new earth (Rev. 21:1).

2. His dignity (2:6)

This psalm of David (Ps. 8:4-6), quoted here (2:6-8a), paradoxically presents the dignity and the insignificance of man simultaneously. The verse before the quotation in Hebrews reads, "When I consider thy heavens, the work of thy fingers, the moon and the stars, which thou hast ordained" (Ps. 8:3). David, as a man, candidly saw the smallness of man in the midst of an immeasurable, magnificent universe. He later was amazed at the brevity of man's life against the infinite, eternal existence of God: "Man is like to vanity: his days are as a shadow that passeth away" (Ps. 144:4). In spite of these obvious, vast differences, David also confessed that God was vitally interested in the affairs of mankind. God made man in His own image, and man will live eternally, whereas the universe will go out of existence.

In what sense did God have interest in man or visit him? The Jewish rabbis did not view Psalm 8 as messianic. Christ however quoted from the psalm to justify His reception of praise by the children in the temple (Matt. 21:16; cf. Ps. 8:2). He often used the title "Son of man" of Himself, yet the people ignorantly queried, "Who is this Son of man?" (John 12:34). Paul identified Him in these words: "the second man is the Lord from heaven" (I Cor. 15:47). The dignity of man, thus, can be seen in the fact that God loved man, that God was concerned about the sinful condition of man, that God visited mankind by becoming human in Christ, that He redeemed man, and that He has reestablished mankind through Christ as the proper rulers of the earth.

3. His purposes (2:7–8)

Four assertions are made. First, God made man "a little lower than the angels."[8] There is a definite order within the universe: God—angels—man—animals—plants—inanimate objects. Angels are spirit beings with power and speed which excel that of humans. They do not die. On the other hand, men are physical-psychical beings in which the material body and the immaterial spirit bear a close relationship. The separation of the two brings death. Men are limited to life on earth in their present bodies, whereas angels function in all three spheres of the heavens plus the earth.

Second, God crowned man "with glory and honor." Man is

8. The Hebrew text of Psalm 8 has "Elohim" (God) rather than "angels." The Septuagint has the reading of "angels." Both the Targum and Jewish commentators render it as "angels."

"the image and glory of God" (I Cor. 11:7). In the scheme of creation, God is more like man than He is like angels. Truth about the being of God can be learned from a study of man. The life of man has honor in that it is precious and bears the image of God. Capital punishment is based upon this value judgment (Gen. 9:6).

Third, God set man "over the works of [His] hands." Man was created on the sixth day, not on any previous day. Man was created after everything else was made. God's creative decree stated: "Let us make man in our image, after our likeness: and let them have dominion over the fish of the sea, and over the fowl of the air, and over the cattle, and over all the earth, and over every creeping thing that creepeth upon the earth" (Gen. 1:26). No angel was given this dominion, either before or after the rebellion of angels led by Lucifer, who became Satan. Man's destiny was to rule. God, being God, always rules. It is His divine prerogative. This charge for man, therefore, represented part of the image of God in man.

Fourth, God "put all things in subjection" under man. He constituted the nature of fish, fowl, animals, and plants to be under the control of man (Gen. 1:26–31; Ps. 8:7–8). God excluded nothing from the domain of man.

Adam, the representative man, lost that original dominion through his sin in the Garden of Eden. The ground became cursed and domestic animals became ferocious (Gen. 3:17–19). The author concludes: "But now we see not yet all things put under him."[9] Man's partial dominion today is gained by difficult work and perseverance.

B. The Provision of Christ (2:9–18)

The previous section ended with a note of defeat and depression. The loss and sin of man, however, are now offset by the triumphant chord of Christ's presence: "But we see Jesus" (2:9a). Emphasis in this passage will focus on the achievements of

9. Some believe that the pronoun "him" refers to Christ, not to man in general. P. E. Hughes, *A Commentary on the Epistle to the Hebrews,* (Grand Rapids: Eerdmans, 1977), p. 86.

Christ through His incarnation, death, resurrection, and ascension. He did this not for Himself, but as the second man, He did it for the benefit of mankind.

1. He became man (2:9a)

Christ "was made a little lower than the angels." He naturally existed before His incarnation. He chose to identify Himself with the human race rather than with the angelic order. He became human, not angelic. He came to earth to die for the sin of mankind only, not for the sin of fallen angels who actually sinned before men did.

2. He died for men (2:9b)

God is self-existent. He has life in Himself. He is not dependent upon anyone or anything outside of Himself for the continuance of His infinite, eternal Being. God, obviously, cannot die.

God thus had to become man in order to experience death and to gain victory over the penalty of sin through death. Five aspects of that event are enumerated here. First, it involved "the suffering of death." It embraced physical agony, psychological abuse, and judicial separation from the Father. Christ predicted that He had to suffer (Matt. 16:21). That announcement confused and saddened the disciples (Matt. 16:22; 17:23). The Old Testament prophets likewise could not understand the relationship between the sufferings of the Messiah and His glorious reign (I Peter 1:11).

Second, Christ was "crowned with glory and honour" at the cross. Man originally had glory and honor because of his distinctiveness within the created order, but Christ, as the representative divine–human person, displayed the greater glory of God through the provision of redemption (John 12:23, 28). The value of man, marked by honor through creation in the image of God, has been heightened through crucifixion.

Third, Christ manifested "the grace of God" in His death. He became man and died for man, even though man did not deserve this love and mercy (Eph. 2:1–10).

46

Fourth, Christ totally experienced death. The force behind "tasted" (*geusētai*) is not a mere sample, a slight touch of the lip or tongue. It connotes total appropriation of the experience, from the beginning to the end. The verbal concept is used elsewhere of physical death (Mark 9:1), of eating food (Luke 14:24), and of salvation through faith (I Peter 2:3). Christ experienced physical death, the separation of the self from the body. In addition, He went through the second death, the separation of a person from God. He died to remove the penalty of both deaths from the destiny of man. This was necessary in order to restore man to his future dominion.

Fifth, Christ died "for every man." His atonement was substitutionary and unlimited (Mark 10:45; I Tim. 2:6; I John 2:2). He died for both Jews and Gentiles, for both men and women. Just as the sin of the first man influenced the entire race, so the death of Christ made a universal provision for deliverance. Its value, of course, must be received by personal faith.

3. He is the leader (2:10)

Christ is the "captain" (*archēgon*) of man's salvation. This compound Greek term is made up of two concepts: to rule and to lead. Christ thus can rule redeemed men because only He can lead them through death, resurrection, and exaltation. The term is translated elsewhere of Christ as "prince" (Acts 3:15; 5:31) and "author" (Heb. 12:2).

Three features of His leadership are cited. First, He had to be made "perfect through sufferings." The meaning of "perfect" (*teleiōsai*) is to bring to a desired end. His human experience could only be completed through the sufferings of death. Christ had no need of ethical perfection, but He did become incarnate in order to fulfill the divine purpose in His crucifixion.

Second, Christ became the leader by whom the Father could bring "many sons unto glory." The "glory" is the full expression of the purpose of God for man through creation and redemption (2:7, 9). In the exaltation of regenerated man throughout eternity, the merger of created glory in Adam (2:7) and the redemptive glory in Christ (2:9) are finalized.

Third, the leadership of Christ is according to God's purpose ("For it became him"). The Father is both the cause ("for whom are all things") and the agent ("by whom are all things") of creation and salvation.[10] The death of Christ, therefore, was according to "the determinate counsel and foreknowledge of God" (Acts 2:23). To achieve leadership perfection, Christ voluntarily came to do that divine will (10:5-7). His human body became the vehicle for suffering and death.

4. He is the brother (2:11-13)

Christ is "he that sanctifieth" (10:10; 13:12; Eph. 5:26). He does it by His blood and His Word. Believers are "they who are sanctified" (10:10, 14; I Cor. 1:2). The verb "sanctify" (*hagiazō*) means "to set apart." It can apply to four different stages of the believer's salvation. It refers to the ministry of the Holy Spirit in the person's life before conversion (Gal. 1:15; II Thess. 2:13); the time of regeneration (I Cor. 1:2; 6:11); the present cleansing of the Christian (John 17:17); and the total separation from the effects of sin when the believer receives the incorruptible, immortal body (Eph. 5:26-27).

Both Christ and the believers "are all of one." Both, in their humanity, can name God as their Father. Within the Trinitarian oneness of the divine Being, there is an eternal Father-Son relationship; in addition, the Father has begotten the Son in the incarnation (1:6; Luke 1:35). A sinful man can become a child of God through spiritual regeneration (Gal. 4:6). This sameness and difference in the relationship to the Father can be detected in Christ's words: "I ascend unto my Father, and your Father" (John 20:17).

Christ's identification with humanity creates the brother-brother relationship. Since both have the Father as their Father, "he is not ashamed to call them brethren."

A series of three quotations from the Old Testament follows to reinforce the brotherly link. The first is from a Davidic, messianic psalm where the sufferings of David typify the suffer-

10. The two prepositions are: "for" (*dia* with the accusative) and "by" (*dia* with the genitive).

ings of the Messiah on the cross (2:12; Ps. 22:22). The praise of God comes after the suffering of the Messiah for His people. Just as David identified himself with the believing remnant who supported his kingship, so the Son of David joins Himself to the believers of today.

The second quotation comes from a prophecy in Isaiah where the prophet puts his trust in God for the deliverance of Israel from her enemies (2:13a; Isa. 8:17). Earlier Isaiah appealed to Israel to sanctify the Lord and to acknowledge Him as their "stone of stumbling" and "rock of offence" (Isa. 8:13-14; I Peter 2:8).

The third is a reference to Isaiah and his two children as signs to Israel (2:13b; Isa. 8:18). They typify Christ and believers in their mutual relationship to God. Believers are God's gifts to His Son (John 6:37) just as God gave children to Isaiah.

5. He destroyed Satan (2:14)

All humans share a common nature; they are "partakers of flesh and blood." These descriptive nouns speak of human life in a physical body wherein the life in the blood animates the material organism. In the Incarnation, Christ "took part of the same." He was a divine person with a divine nature, but He obtained a perfect and complete human nature through the virgin conception. He thus had human life in its total expression, yet apart from sin (Luke 2:52).

In His theanthropic person, one person with two natures, Christ could now shed His blood, the very essence of physical life. He had to go "through death" to destroy Satan. He had to go through death to make the resurrection possible. After the sin of Adam, God announced to Satan that the seed of the woman would bruise his head and that the devil would bruise the heel of the seed (Gen. 3:15). That prophecy was fulfilled at the Crucifixion. At the cross, Christ judged and defeated Satan (John 12:31; 16:11). The verb "destroy" (katargēsēi) means "to render inoperative."

What is "the power of death" that Satan possessed? Negatively, it is not the authority to kill people. God has that power (Gen. 2:17; Matt. 10:28). Positively, it is the power to keep men in the realm of physical death after they have died. The penalty of sin is both physical and spiritual death. Christ had to die physically to go into the realm of death and hades, and to come out via resurrection. Today Christ has the keys of death and hades (Rev. 1:18). His resurrection guarantees the resurrection of all believers so that they might share in His ultimate dominion.

6. He delivered the fearful (2:15)

The "fear of death" could refer to the experience of dying, the concern that there is no life after death or no resurrection after death, or to eternal separation from God in the lake of fire. The believer does not need to have any of these fears since Christ conquered death in all of its forms through His crucifixion and resurrection.

Christ came to set men free from moral bondage (John 8:32, 36). An understanding of this precious truth will also produce psychological freedom. Spiritual sonship carries no corollary of bondage (Gal. 4:1–7).

The fact that there is a resurrected human being in heaven should bring spiritual assurance and hope. Christ's immortal, incorruptible body is a guarantee that all believers will have the same type of body when He comes to raise the dead. They also can have the joy that they go directly into the presence of Christ upon their deaths (II Cor. 5:8; Phil. 1:23).

The verb "deliver" (apallassō) is used elsewhere of deliverance from an accuser (Luke 12:58) and from diseases through miraculous healing (Acts 19:12).

7. He became a Jew (2:16)

Here is a contrast between the angels and the patriarch Abraham. Christ did not become an angel to deliver the fallen angels from their sin and punishment. Contrariwise, He took on Him "the seed of Abraham." Elsewhere, Paul declared that He "was made of the seed of David according to the flesh" (Rom. 1:3).

The meaning of the verb "took" (*epilambanetai*) is debatable. It is used later of God, who took Israel by the hand to lead them out of their bondage in Egypt (8:9; cf. Jer. 31:9). In that context it has the sense of assistance, help, and deliverance. Thus, does this verse simply teach that Christ came to help Israel? But what was the channel of that assistance? To deliver Israel, the physical seed or posterity of Abraham, He had to become humanly the Son of David, the son of Abraham (Matt. 1:1). The assistance, consequently, came through the Incarnation by Mary, who could trace her genealogical record back to David, Abraham, and Adam (Luke 3:23–38).

The provision of redemption for the human race had to be made by the singular "seed of Abraham," namely Christ (Gal. 3:16). God's unconditional promise to Abraham stated: ". . .in thee shall all families of the earth be blessed" (Gen. 12:3).

8. He became a high priest (2:17a)

Here is the first mention of Christ's high priesthood in the book. Three aspects are given here. First, He had "to be made like unto his brethren." The likeness (*homoiōthēnai*) does not imply that He was less than a real man. It means that Christ appeared as real men appear. He walked and talked like ordinary men; He did not have a halo around His head nor did a glow emanate from His body. Paul said that He came to be "in the likeness of men" (Phil. 2:7). He came "in the likeness of sinful flesh" (Rom. 8:3). Christ neither inherited nor obtained a sin nature; nevertheless, His humanity was just as perfect and complete as that of any man. Priests can be taken only from other members of the human race (5:1). Christ thus had to become human in order to qualify for the position.

Second, He was "merciful." Many first-century high priests, such as Annas and Caiaphas, served Rome and their own selfish interests. Christ, in contrast, was full of compassion and sympathy for the needs of the people.

Third, Christ was "faithful" to God in the administration of His priestly functions. His life was marked by fidelity, devotion, and a total commitment to the task.

9. He made a propitiation (2:17b)

Christ made a propitiatory sacrifice "for the sins of the people." The term "propitiation" is a better rendering than "reconciliation." The Greek term (*hilaskesthai*) is used elsewhere of the sacrifice of Christ which completely satisfied the righteous demands of God for sin (Rom. 3:25; I John 2:2). The place of propitiation was the "mercy seat," a word built upon this Greek term (9:5). On the Day of Atonement which occurred only once each year, the high priest of Israel would go into the Most Holy Place and sprinkle the blood of sacrifice upon the mercy seat that sat on the ark of the covenant. The cross literally became the place of sacrifice and propitiation.

10. He can help men (2:18)

As the result of His incarnation and crucifixion, Christ is able to "succour" or help men. The verb "succour" (*boēthēsai*) is a compound term based upon the words "cry" (*boē*) and "run" (*theō*). The descriptive analogy, thus, is to run to the assistance of a person who is crying out for help. Christ did just that.

The ones who need help are "them that are tempted." It is not wrong or sinful to be tempted, but it is wrong to yield to the temptation. Christ's assistance comes at the time the person is being tempted.[11] The help is available so that the believer can overcome the test. The essence behind temptation is to act independently of the revealed will of God. When a child of God yields his will to the divine, he then gains the victory.

There are two reasons why Christ has ability to help. First, He Himself was "tempted." Both in the threefold temptation of Satan at the outset of Christ's ministry (Matt. 4:1–11) and in the Garden of Gethsemane at the conclusion of His earthly work (Matt. 26:36–46), there was temptation to reject the will of God. Christ thus knows what temptation is all about.

Second, Christ "suffered." He went through the same moral, physical, and psychological anguish that men experience. Christ had victory in the temptation to avoid the cross and its total

11. The verbal form ("are tempted") is a present passive participle.

implications. The author wants his readers to receive the help of Christ when they are tempted to avoid identification with the Savior.

Questions for Discussion

1. How can believers be more attentive to revealed truth? How can church services help or hinder?

2. What types of judgments can come upon believers who reject truth? Are they always evident to others?

3. Can miracles occur today? What is a real biblical miracle? Are all spiritual gifts temporary or permanent?

4. What areas of life are under the dominion of man today? Which are exempt?

5. What are the characteristics of spiritual brotherhood? With each other? With Christ?

6. Why do some believers fear death? How can they be helped?

7. What kind of assistance is needed when a person is being tempted? Can a person prepare for a test before it happens?

3

Christ, Moses, and Israel
Hebrews 3:1–19

The superiority of Christ to the prophets (1:1–3) and to the angels (1:4—2:18) has been clearly demonstrated. Since the angels were the supernatural agents in the giving of the law, the significance of the human agent, namely Moses, must also be studied. In chapter 3, the author vividly proves the superiority of Christ to Moses and then issues a warning to his readers.

I. CHRIST IS BETTER THAN MOSES (3:1–6)

The inferential conjunction "wherefore" (*hothen*) joins together the two sections (3:1–19 with 1:1—2:18). It especially points to the discussion of Christ in His various works (2:9–18).

The readers are then described in four ways. This is the first time that they are addressed directly in the book. Their characterization definitely shows that the author regarded them as saved people. First, they are "brethren." They are brothers to the author and brothers to Christ (2:11–13). The term "brother" (*adelphos*), in derivation, means "from the same womb" (*apo* and *delphus*). Their spiritual origin was from the womb of God through regeneration. They are later addressed as brethren (3:12; 10:19; 13:22). He also mentions Timothy as their common brother (13:23).

Second, they are "holy." This term (*hagioi*) can be used either as an adjective ("holy") or as a substantive ("saints"). It is translated elsewhere in the book as "saints" (6:10; 13:24). Holy persons are saints, and saints are holy persons. They literally are "set apart ones," or "sanctified ones." Their theological sanctification was discussed earlier (2:11). The term basically describes the spiritual position of a genuine believer, not the practice of his life.

Third, they are "partakers of the heavenly calling." The noun "partakers" (*metochoi*) comes from a verb which means "to have with." It was used of Christ who "took part" of the nature of man (2:14). The noun is applied later to the readers as they are partakers of Christ (3:14), of the Holy Spirit (6:4), and of divine chastisement for erring children (12:8). In a nontheological passage, the fishing "partners" of Peter are so described (Luke 5:7). The term thus involves full participation. The readers were partakers of the "heavenly calling." This refers to the efficacious call of God whereby He always brings those sinners to Himself whom He has chosen from eternity past (I Cor. 1:2, 26). The readers are later designated as "the called," who will receive the divine inheritance (9:15). God thus is the one who calls, and the called are those who respond in saving faith. The calling then becomes the standard by which believers should govern their conduct (Eph. 4:1; Phil. 3:14). The call is "heavenly" in both origin and destination. The heavenly God calls earthly men to a heavenly eternity and presently bestows on them a plethora of heavenly blessings (Eph. 1:3). The promise of God includes for the readers a heavenly country (11:16) and a heavenly city, new Jerusalem (12:22).

Fourth, the readers were people who confessed their faith publicly. The noun "profession" (*homologias*) can also be translated "confession." It literally means "same word." A confession, therefore, means to say the same thing as someone else. The term is used twice more in this book (4:14; 10:23) and only three times elsewhere (II Cor. 9:13; I Tim. 6:12, 13), but always of believers. The verbal form is employed often of the confession of men unto salvation (Matt. 10:32; John 9:22; Rom. 10:9–10). The mention of "our" confession shows that the author regarded the profession of the readers to be of the same nature as his.

The appeal to the readers was a direct, simple command: "consider" (*katanoēsate*). The compound word literally means "mind down." To consider is to put one's mind down on an object or person. It involves reflective study, attentive examination, and careful thought. The immaturity and insecurity of the readers were caused by an unhealthy preoccupation of self and problems. The moral remedy was an active meditation on the merit of Christ in His person and redemptive work. The verbal command is used later for a consideration of the needs of other believers (10:24).

A. As an Apostle and High Priest (3:1)

1. The apostle

Christ is seen in two ways. First, He is "the apostle" (*ton apostolon*). It is the same word used of Paul and the twelve. It depicts one who is sent by an authoritative head to do something with the full investment of power. In its noun form, it is only used here of Christ; however, the verbal form is employed often to show that God the Father sent the Son to reveal God and to perform the work of redemption (John 3:17; 20:21; I John 4:10). The Savior Himself commented, "And this is life eternal, that they might know thee, the only true God, and Jesus Christ, whom thou hast sent [same word]" (John 17:3). The confession of a believing sinner, therefore, includes the conviction that Christ was sent by God into this world. This fact would be an admission of His deity and a denial of the heresy that Christ was a mere man.

2. The high priest

Second, Christ is the "high priest," not just a priest in the midst of many other priests. A high priest is literally "a priest who rules" (*archierea*). He rules over other priests and the priestly system of sacrifice and worship. In function he represented the interests of the people before their God. He alone could go before God on the Day of Atonement to sprinkle the blood of

56

the sacrifice on the mercy seat. In the confession of salvation, therefore, a believing sinner must admit the humanity of Christ, the sacrifice of His life and the shedding of His blood, and the total commitment to Christ as His only means to God.

The usage of the two terms together manifest Christ's deity and humanity. They show His ministry of revealing and redeeming. In the analogy with the Old Testament, He incorporated into Himself the two ministries of Moses and Aaron. Moses was the apostle sent by God from Sinai to reveal the law to Israel, whereas Aaron was the nation's first high priest, who represented the people before God in the Holy of Holies within the tabernacle.

B. As a Builder (3:2-4)

The analogy of house construction now begins. Obvious contrasts are made between the builder and the house and between the resident and the servant in that house.

1. Christ is more faithful (3:2)

Christ is "faithful." Earlier He was called a faithful High Priest (2:17). Faithfulness involves obedience to do an appointed task—to do it in the prescribed way, to do it well, to do it at the right time, and to do it out of a loving spirit. It involves integrity and moral resolution. It is an indispensable qualification for stewardship (I Cor. 4:2). Faithful men are the custodians of trust. Christ came to do the will of God, and He did it in the divinely appointed way. Only He could say: ". . .for I do always those things that please him" (John 8:29).

Christ's faithfulness was directed toward the Father, namely "to him that appointed him." God appointed the Son to the task of revealing Apostle and redeeming High Priest. The same verb (poieō) is used of the appointment of the Twelve to become apostles (Mark 3:14), of the authentication of Jesus as Lord and Christ (Acts 2:36), and of the assignment of believers as kings and priests (Rev. 1:6).

Moses was faithful in "all his house." The term "house" refers to that place of divine manifestation wherein men serve God. In the time of Moses the nation of Israel was the people wherein God dwelled. He marked His presence with the glory inside the tabernacle, the guiding cloud by day, and the pillar of fire by night. Moses' sphere of ministry was within the people of Israel. When Miriam and Aaron led a rebellion against the exclusive leadership, God responded with this commendation of Moses: "My servant Moses is not so, who is faithful in all mine house" (Num. 12:7). His faithfulness, however, was not total and permanent. It was marred by subsequent disobedience and divine chastisement. When Moses smote the rock a second time instead of speaking to it, God said to him: "Because ye believed me not, to sanctify me in the eyes of the children of Israel, therefore ye shall not bring this congregation into the land which I have given them" (Num. 20:12). Moses' faithfulness became faithlessness. Christ thus is better than Moses in the sphere of faithfulness.

2. Christ has more glory (3:3–4)

The principle is clear. The builder of the house has "more honor than the house." A person has more value than his property. Christ is the builder in the analogy, and the church is the house. After His rejection by the religious leaders, Christ announced a new program: "I will build my church." The church of this age is composed of saved Jews and saved Gentiles, made one in Christ through the baptism in the Holy Spirit (I Cor. 12:13). The church is equated with Christ's body (Eph. 1:22–23; 5:23, 30–32). It is also identified as "the house of God, which is the church of the living God, the pillar and ground of the truth" (I Tim. 3:15).

Christ also "has more glory than Moses." Moses did not build the nation of Israel; God started that people with the call of Abraham. Moses, as an Israelite, faithfully served within Israel for forty years, or one-third of his natural life.

Christ thus has more glory and honor. These very terms

described the significance of His crucifixion. At that time He was "crowned with glory and honour" (2:9).

Every effect must have an adequate cause, thus "every house is builded by some man." The ultimate builder, however, is the Trinitarian God.[1]

C. As the Son (3:5–6)

1. Moses was a servant (3:5)

Moses had positive qualities. First, he is again described as "faithful in all his house." His leadership and contribution to his own generation must be praised.

Second, Moses was faithful "as a servant." Moses recorded that God called him a servant (Num. 12:7). This distinctive term for a servant (*theropōn*)[2] is based upon the verb "to heal." Moses' service was in a ministry of moral and spiritual healing, prescribing positive areas of nutrition and eliminating the destructive elements. He did what he could in the best interests of the national health of Israel. As great as he was, though, he was still just a servant.

Third, Moses' ministry was preparatory. What he said and wrote were "for a testimony of those things which were to be spoken after." God spoke to Moses "mouth to mouth" (Num. 12:8), and Moses passed the truth on to the people. In the Book of Hebrews we see that God has spoken by prophets, angels, and Moses; however, all of their ministries anticipated the greater revelation of God in Christ. Christ challenged His critics to search the Old Testament Scriptures (John 5:39), then He added, "For had ye believed Moses, ye would have believed me: for he wrote of me" (v. 46). The typology of the tabernacle and the sacrificial system foreshadowed the reality of Christ's person and redemptive work. He was the Passover lamb (I Cor. 5:7); He was the mercy seat (Rom. 3:25); and He was the veil of the inner sanctuary (10:20). Countless other types and analogies can be

1. The noun "God" appears without the definite article.
2. Used only here in the New Testament. The word "therapy" comes from it.

carefully gleaned from the Pentateuch. After His resurrection, Christ expounded to the two disciples on the road to Emmaus "things concerning himself" which could be found in "Moses and all the prophets" (Luke 24:27, 44-45).

2. Christ is the Son (3:6)

Moses was a servant *in* His house, the nation of Israel, but Christ is a son *over* His house, the church. A son is superior to a servant, and to be over a house is greater than to be in a house. Christ is the spiritual head of His body, the church (Eph. 1:22-24).

The author then confidently asserted: "...whose house are we." He saw his readers and himself as an integral part of the company of the redeemed of this age (I Cor. 3:9; Gal. 6:10; Eph. 2:19-22; I Peter 4:17).

A contingency, however, is introduced in which the author includes himself with his readers. People do not become the house by holding fast, but they manifest the fact that they are the house by holding fast. The genuineness of saving faith is evident "if we hold fast the confidence and the rejoicing of the hope firm unto the end." Robertson observed, "This note of contingency and doubt runs all through the Epistle."[3] Real saints are the ones who persevere. In fact, God uses the warnings to assist the sensitive believer to remain orthodox. Hughes correctly noted: "Security in Christ does not absolve one from personal responsibility; quite the contrary, for the regenerate man is under total obligation to God. Seriousness in believing should manifest itself in seriousness concerning doctrine and conduct."[4]

The issue in this passage is basically a doctrinal commitment to the total mediatorship of Christ in His redemptive work. The concept of "confidence" (*parrēsian*) means that a believer has complete access to the Father through the Son. The essence of

3. A. T. Robertson, *Word Pictures in the New Testament* (Nashville: Broadman, 1932), V:355.

4. P. E. Hughes, *A Commentary on the Epistle to the Hebrews* (Grand Rapids: Eerdmans, 1977), p. 139.

"rejoicing" consists of the realization that Christ has totally satisfied the righteous demands of God for a person's sins and that his rejoicing rests in the Son (Gal. 6:14; Phil. 3:1). Throughout Scripture there are warnings that deviation from basic soteriological and christological fundamentals reveal that the person's original profession was not genuine (I Cor. 15:1–2; II Cor. 13:5; Col. 1:20–23; I John 2:18–19). The faith that saves is a faith which begins to rest in Christ alone and continues to remain there. Christ Himself said to those who professed belief, "If ye continue in my word, then are ye my disciples indeed" (John 8:31).

II. THE SECOND WARNING (3:7–19)

The conjunction "wherefore" gives the conclusion to the argument for the superiority of Christ over Moses and also introduces a warning to the readers. This conjunction (*dio*) is actually used nine times throughout the epistle (3:7, 10; 6:1; 10:5; 11:12, 16; 12:12, 28; 13:12).

A. The Appeal Stated (3:7–8a)

1. Its source

The appeal takes the form of a quotation from the Old Testament (Ps. 95:7–11). The author of the biblical passage is the Holy Spirit ("as the Holy Spirit saith"). The written statements of the psalm and the words of the Holy Spirit are thus synonymous. A human author naturally used the pen and scroll, but he wrote under the sovereign superintendence of the Spirit. Peter charged that "holy men of God spake as they were moved by the Holy Ghost" (II Peter 1:21). The apostles recognized that the Spirit spoke by the spoken and written words of the prophets (Acts 1:16; 28:25) and that the Spirit likewise authoritatively guided their doctrinal pronouncements (Acts 21:11; I Cor. 2:13; I Tim. 4:1; Rev. 2:7).

61

2. *Its context*

Psalm 95 provides the context from which the author selected the appeal. It begins with an exhortation to believers: "O come, let us sing unto the LORD: Let us make a joyful noise to the rock of our salvation. Let us come before his presence with thanksgiving, and make a joyful noise unto him with psalms" (Ps. 95:1-2). The very verse, which contains the start of the appeal, begins with this assertion: "For he is our God; and we are the people of his pasture, and the sheep of his hand" (Ps. 95:7). The analogy is obvious. The author had just stated that the readers and he were the house of Christ; then he issued the solemn warning which the psalmist had given to the Old Testament believers. The warning, thus, is to genuine children of God. All of the direct imperatives must be interpreted against that conclusion.

3. *Its nature*

Three features can be seen. First, the appeal was urgent. The temporal adverb ("today") shows that the admonition and desired obedience were concurrent. The readers could not deliberate or delay their response.

Second, the success of the appeal was based upon a sensitive audience ("if you will hear his voice"). The hearing involved more than just passive listening; it also included an active willingness to obey even before the command was given. Christ often charged, "Who hath ears to hear, let him hear" (Matt. 13:43). Unfortunately rebels hear but do not understand (Matt. 13:15).

Third, the appeal was a prohibition: "Harden not your hearts." Of the six times this verb is used in the New Testament, four occur in this book (3:8, 13, 15; 4:7). The prohibition may be against either the beginning or the ending of the hardening process.[5] The sense thus could be: Don't begin to harden, or don't allow hardening to get to that point where you are no longer responsive to God. A hardened substance is that which

5. *Mē sklērunēte.* Respectively, either an ingressive aorist or a culminative aorist.

dries up or becomes stiff. Each act of disobedience simply produces another layer of spiritual callousness.

B. The Historical Illustration (3:8b–11)

The dilemma of the readers is equated with the wilderness experience of the children of Israel. That was a period of forty years, dating from the exodus from Egyptian bondage under the leadership of Moses to the entrance into Canaan under the direction of Joshua.

1. The sin of Israel

Their sin is called "the provocation" (*toi parapikrasmōi*). The word literally means "beside or beyond bitterness." It is used only three times in the New Testament, always of Israel (3:8, 15, 16). It doubtless embraces the murmuring, the complaints, and the exasperation which their bitter spirits produced. They be-came dissatisfied with God's leadership and provision. At Re-phidim where the Israelites had no water, they questioned God's presence and goodness (Exod. 17:1–7). At Marah they murmured because the water was bitter (Exod. 15:23–26). In the wilderness of Sin, they griped because they had no bread (Exod. 16:1–4). They then tired of the manna and complained because they had no meat (Num. 11:10–25). They again screamed that they had no water at Zin (Num. 20:1–13).

This provocation occurred "in the day of temptation in the wilderness." The "day," of course, encompassed the entire period of forty years. The "temptation" (*peirasmou*) had two sides. From the divine position, God did test the Israelites. This type of test, however, is always for the spiritual benefit of the recipients (James 1:2–12). From the human side, Israel tempted God in that she refused to trust Him in spite of His miraculous display and then had the audacity to demand more signs. In His indictment of their unbelief, God concluded, "Because all those men which have seen my glory, and my miracles, which I did in the wilderness, and have tempted me now these ten times, and have not hearkened to my voice; surely they shall not see the land. . ." (Num. 14:22-23a). They had indeed provoked God (Num. 14:23b). They tempted and proved God, even though they had seen His works (3:9). They actually sat in judgment of God for forty years.

The period of forty years was also the approximate length of time from the Crucifixion to the writing of Hebrews. These believers were also being tested by God (2:18). The danger was that they might tempt and provoke God as Israel had done.

2. The response of God

Three insights into the divine response are given. First, God "was grieved with that generation." The verb (prosōchthisa)[6] indicates extreme anger and disgust. God was morally incensed over their attitude. When Israel refused to enter the land at Kadesh-barnea, and when they were about to kill Joshua and Caleb for the latter's confidence in God, Jehovah manifested Himself with this reaction:

> . . .And the glory of the Lord appeared in the tabernacle of the congregation before all of the children of Israel.
>
> And the Lord said unto Moses, How long will this people provoke me? and how long will it be ere they believe me, for all the signs which I have shewed among them?
>
> I will smite them with the pestilence, and disinherit them, and will make of thee a greater nation and mightier than they (Num. 14:10-12).

That initial response, however, was balanced by His long-suffering, forgiveness, and faithfulness to the promises of the Abrahamic covenant (Num. 14:18).

Second, God evaluated their sin under two categories. They had heart and head problems: "They do always err in their heart; and they have not known my ways" (3:10). The first denotes an inner propensity toward rebellion, a desire to go astray as lost sheep (Isa. 53:6). The second reveals an ignorance of the divine intent behind His commandments, guidance, and providential control.

6. Used only twice in the New Testament (3:10, 17).

Third, God was full of "wrath" (*orgē*). Holy anger is always the divine response to the deliberate disobedience of God's revealed, righteous will. In wrath He pronounced an irrevocable sentence of chastising judgment upon that adult generation "from twenty years old and upward, which have murmured against me" (Num. 14:29). The rebels could not enter His "rest," a term that described the land of Canaan. During the forty years of wandering, that generation perished in the wilderness (Num. 14:22–23). They did not lose their personal salvation (if they had it), but they did lose the opportunity to move into the place of corporate national blessing.

C. The Appeal Repeated (3:12–19)

The first appeal, illustrated by Israel's failure, is now repeated and reinforced. Five verbal concepts comprise the essence of the admonition.

1. Take heed (3:12)

The direct address ("brethren") again shows the author's conviction that his readers are genuine believers, although he admits the possibility of a few false professors.

The command to "take heed" calls for moral alertness and spiritual vigilance. It literally means "see" or "watch" (*blepete*). It is translated elsewhere as "beware" (Phil. 3:2).

Three features of the warning can be seen. First, it was directed to each individual ("lest there be in any of you"). Here was a concern for one person as well as for the entire group. One person can influence an entire group, for either good or bad.

Second, his interest was over their inner moral disposition. He did not want any of them to develop "an evil heart of unbelief." The nature of the evil would be in the decision not to believe.[7]

---

7. The phrase literally reads: "A heart evil with reference to unbelief" (*kardia ponēra apistias*).

Third, the result of the unbelieving, evil heart would be "in departing from the living God." The term "apostasy" is based upon the verb for departure (*apostēnai*). It literally means "to take a stand away from." The point of departure is God Himself. There is an apostasy of practice which results in the forfeiture of earthly blessing, and there is a doctrinal apostasy which marks the unsaved. Both are prompted by a decision not to believe: the former not to trust God for daily sustenance and the latter not to believe for eternal salvation. The former is under discussion in this verse.

2. Exhort (3:13)

Three aspects of the reciprocal exhortation are given. First, the nature of exhortation is encouragement and comfort. The verb literally means "called beside" (*parakaleite*). The Holy Spirit is the divine Paraclete, the Comforter of all believers (John 14:16–17, 26).

Second, there must be "daily" exhortation as long as the day of grace and longsuffering is in operation ("while it is called Today"). The situation of the readers is thus likened to that of Israel before it made its irreversible decision at Kadesh.

Third, the desired result of exhortation is the prohibition of spiritual hardening. God did not want any individual to be hardened through the deceitfulness of sin. The Greek here literally reads "the sin" (*tēs hamartias*) and refers to the specific sin of unbelief (3:12). Sin can also deceive through riches (Matt. 13:22), lusts (Eph. 4:22), philosophy (Col. 2:8), and unrighteousness (II Thess. 2:10).

3. Hold fast (3:14)

The evidence of salvation is again doctrinal integrity and perseverance. There is a switch in address from the second person ("you") to the first person ("we"). The first part of the verse contains a statement of fact: "For we are made partakers of Christ." The verb (*gegonamen*) denotes both the event and the results of regeneration.[8] The noun "partakers" earlier described the readers (3:1).

8. Perfect active indicative.

66

How can a person determine whether he really was saved at a given place and time? The answer is found in the conditional clause: ". . .if we hold the beginning of our confidence stedfast unto the end." The term "beginning" (*hupostaseōs*) literally means "that which stands under." It is the foundation of salvation, namely the conviction that Christ is both divine and human and that He died for sins and rose again. Faith permeates that foundation (Heb. 11:1). If a professing Christian subsequently denies the deity of Christ or the efficacy of His death, then that denial demonstrates that he had never become a genuine partaker of Christ. Robertson reported that Jonathan Edwards once said that "the sure proof of election is that one holds out to the end."[9]

4. Harden not (3:15–17)

The historical illustration of Israel in the wilderness is again used to prompt the repetition of the prohibition against hardening (3:15). God, however, did discriminate between the faithful and the unfaithful within the corporate body of Israel. A distinction is made between the individual and the nation ("not all that came out of Egypt by Moses"). The rebels were those who heard the truth (3:16), hardened their hearts (3:15), provoked God (3:16), grieved Him (3:17), sinned (3:17), and died in the wilderness (3:17).

It should not be surmised that every Israelite who died between Egypt and Canaan was a rebel or unsaved. Moses, Aaron, and Miriam were buried outside of the Promised Land, and no one would doubt their salvation. Unfortunately, the nation suffered as a whole because of the judgment of God upon the rebels.

5. Believe (3:18–19)

Those who "believed not" did not enter the rest of Canaan (3:18).

9. Robertson, *Word Pictures,* pp. 338–39.

The conclusion of this section is now introduced by the inferential words ("so we see"). It is apparent to all. The problem was "unbelief" (3:19).

Christ came to give both life and abundant life (John 10:10). Saving faith secures life (John 3:16), but walking faith appropriates the essence and abundance of eternal life. All saved people possess the first type of faith, but only some have the second. Many Christians simply exist or survive their earthly sojourn, wandering around in the wilderness of frustration, lack of fulfillment, and self-pity. Few claim their divine inheritance which can be enjoyed now. Without such faith, it is impossible to please God (11:6).

Questions for Discussion

1. How does God call men to Himself? How do divine calling and human responsibility function together?

2. What is involved in a genuine confession of faith? How should it be done? Publicly? Privately?

3. Define faithfulness. How can a believer become faithful? How can faith be observed and tested?

4. How can the warning passages be used to argue for eternal security? To argue against eternal security?

5. How can believers tempt God? Anger Him? Grieve Him?

6. How does lack of faith begin in the life of a Christian? How can it be corrected?

7. What are the characteristics of the abundant life? How is it gained? Lost? Regained?

4

The Rest of God
Hebrews 4:1–16

Paul asserted that the experiences of Israel recorded in the Old Testament serve as examples or types to contemporary believers. He then added that "they are written for our admonition, upon whom the ends of the world are come" (I Cor. 10:11). A familiar axiom states that experience is the best teacher, but pedagogical experts know that learning begins within the desire of the student. Someone has observed that those who are ignorant of history are bound to repeat it. When students have an insatiable appetite for wisdom, they can then learn not only from their own limited experiences, but also from those of others. Believers must do likewise.

This chapter serves as a transition. The first part will conclude the various contrasts between Christ and the Old Testament spokesmen (4:1–13). The closing verses will serve as a fitting introduction to the lengthy comparison between Christ's priesthood and that of the tribe of Levi (4:14–16).

I. THE THIRD WARNING (4:1–11)

The third warning builds upon the second. The second focused on Moses and the ill-fated decision at Kadesh, whereas the third stresses Joshua and the entrance into Canaan. The conjunction ("therefore") joins the two. This passage begins with an exhortation (4:1), and it ends with one (4:11).

A. The Exhortation to Fear (4:1-8)

The significant noun "rest" occurs eight times in Hebrews (3:11, 18; 4:1, 3 [twice], 5, 10, 11) and only once elsewhere (Acts 7:49). Its verbal form is used three times in this book (4:4, 8, 10) and only once in the other books of the New Testament (Acts 14:18). Based upon the verb "to cease" (*pauomai*), it literally means "to cease down" or "to thoroughly cease" (*katapausis*). The emphasis of this chapter, therefore, is on the subject of rest, since that concept is mentioned nine times in it.

1. The loss of rest (4:1)

Three aspects of this possible forfeiture can be seen. First, a believer should be marked by fear as he contemplates the consequences of his spiritual decisions. The author included himself with his readers in this self-directed exhortation ("let us fear").[1] Fear can be either good or bad. God has not given to believers "the spirit of fear, but of power, and of love, and of a sound mind" (II Tim. 1:7). They should not fear the threats of unsaved men (Matt. 10:28), the criticism of legalistic religionists (Gal. 2:12), or the removal of divine love and forgiveness (I John 4:18). On the other hand, a Christian wife should fear her husband (Eph. 5:33) and all believers should have *theophobia,* a genuine fear of God (Matt. 10:28). Such awe and reverent respect constitute the "beginning of knowledge" (Prov. 1:7). All should perfect holiness in the fear of God (II Cor. 7:1). All should work out their own salvation "with fear and trembling" (Phil. 2:12).

Israel failed at Kadesh because they feared the inhabitants of Canaan rather than God. Their fright of men clouded their fear of God. Believers should never be afraid of God because He is their Father, but they ought to fear Him because He is their Creator and Redeemer.

Second, loss comes from a failure to believe the promise of God. God is faithful to His promise (10:23). The justification of Abraham by faith provides the pattern for all future believers:

1. It is a hortatory subjunctive, aorist passive (*phobēthōmen*).

70

He staggered not at the promise of God through unbelief; but was strong in faith, giving glory to God;

And being fully persuaded that, what He had promised, he was able also to perform.

And therefore it was imputed to him for righteousness (Rom. 4:20–22).

God promised to give the land of Canaan to Abraham and his physical posterity (Gen. 12:1, 7; 13:14–16). Prior to the entrance of Israel into Canaan under Joshua, God again repeated His promise (Josh. 1:2–4). The people, however, expressed at Kadesh their unbelief in the power of God to perform what He had promised to the patriarchs. The earthly enjoyment of the divine promise was contingent upon their willingness to believe and to act in obedience. In this age God has promised the abundant life to those who have come out of their own spiritual bondage. The enjoyment of that promise is based upon an entrance, a forward movement in trust.

Third, the possibility of failure was imminent. It is indicated by the negative result clause: "lest . . . any of you should seem to come short of it." At the time of writing, no reader had actually apostasized. The verb ("seems") suggests that the resemblance to the decision of Israel at Kadesh was beginning to manifest itself. The readers had not yet decided. Their immaturity and spiritual hesitation were not good signs, however. This was the main reason why the author gave this exhortation on fear. It was a warning to encourage advance while there was still time. He wanted them to have the abundant life, not "to come short of it."

2. The requirements for rest (4:2–3)

Two requirements are necessary for rest. The first is to hear the gospel message. Hearing takes place before believing (Rom. 10:14, 17). The noun "gospel" does not appear in this verse, nor at all in this book. The verbal form ("evangelize") only occurs twice (4:2, 6). This verse literally begins: "We are evangelized people" (*esmen euēggelismenoi*).[2] A saved person is always an

2. Periphrastic construction using the perfect passive participle with the present of *eimi*.

evangelized person, but every evangelized person is not neces-sarily saved. The author included himself again with his readers as the objects of the evangelistic efforts of others. The term "gospel" means "a good message" or "good news." The gospel of salvation was first preached by Christ and then by the apostles (2:3).

At Kadesh, the nation heard the gospel from the twelve spies who were sent by Moses into the land (Num. 13). They returned with the fruit of the land, agreed that the land flowed "with milk and honey," and announced that giants and high walled cities were there. When ten spies testified that the Canaanites were stronger than the Israelites, the people lamented and com-plained. The other two spies, Joshua and Caleb, then gave this positive witness:

> ...The land, which we passed through to search it, is an exceeding good land.
>
> If the Lord delight in us, then he will bring us into this land, and give it to us; a land which floweth with milk and honey.
>
> Only rebel not ye against the LORD, neither fear ye the people of the land; for they are bread for us: their defence is departed from them, and the LORD is with us: fear them not (Num. 14:7-9).

The second requirement for entrance is faith. The rebels at Kadesh heard the word, but it was not "mixed with faith." They did not share the confidence of Joshua and Caleb. They feared man and did not trust God. They did not believe that the God who had saved them out of Egyptian bondage could deliver them from the giants of Canaan. They had trusted God in their past, but they could not trust Him for their future. They treated the testimony of the two godly spies as the opinion of mere men, not as the authoritative message of divinely sent spokes-men (cf. I Thess. 2:13).

The author then confidently asserted his conviction about himself and his readers: "For we which have believed do enter into rest. . . ." Their faith happened in the past at the event of regeneration, and they were presently going forward in their spiritual experience. He did not say that they had already entered into the rest. Note the difference between the past tense ("believed") and the present ("do enter"). The rest was still future for all of them (4:11).

A distinction is then made between the salvation rest and the creation rest (4:3b). God, through the psalmist (Ps. 95:11), announced the existence of a future rest even though He had already begun His rest after His work of creation (Gen. 2:1-3).

3. The meaning of rest (4:4-5)

This passage speaks of two kinds of rest: the creation rest (4:4) and the salvation rest (4:5). The first, the creation rest, is based upon the creative week described in Genesis. God created the world, the heaven and the earth and all that is in them, in six days (Gen. 1:1-31; Exod. 20:11). On the seventh day, He rested from "all his works," namely His creative activity, but He continued His work of sustaining His universe. God's work week produced a pattern for Israel to follow. One of the Ten Commandments prohibited work on the last day of the week (Exod. 20:8-11). The Sabbath thus became a distinctive sign of Israel's covenant relationship to God (Exod. 31:12-18). Obedience demonstrated a faith that God would physically sustain them for seven days even though they had worked only six. The Sabbath was a symbol of trust.

The quotation (Gen. 2:2) shows that what God spoke ("he spake") can be seen in what Moses wrote ("in a certain place"). It is a reinforcement of the doctrine of the verbal plenary inspiration of the Scriptures.

The second rest, the salvation rest, is implied in the second quotation (4:5; Ps. 95:11). It was spoken of in the time of David (4:7), definitely later than the period of Moses and Joshua. The "rest," of course, could not refer to the creation rest or to the rest of Canaan. The offer of entrance into salvation is a challenge to trust God for His completed work of redemption and to live in the enjoyment of those spiritual blessings which are appropriated by faith.

4. The hope of rest (4:6–8)

Four observations can be gleaned from this section. First, the hope of a future entrance into divine rest can be seen in the announcement of God through David ("seeing therefore it remaineth that some must enter therein"). The usage of the pronoun "some" shows that there would be a response to the future invitation, but that it would not be unanimous.

Second, the hope of rest is always based upon faith. At Kadesh, the evangelized Israelites "entered not in because of unbelief." Since some did enter, then the cause of their success must have been the presence of faith in God.

Third, the opportunity of hope is always limited to a specific time and place. For Israel, it was Kadesh. That was their "today" experience. The divine invitation to enter is always gracious, but it can be withdrawn. The meaning of the adverb ("today") thus can be seen in that period when God is speaking and men are hearing His voice. It has always been that way. The wicked heard the voice of God in Noah, the preacher of righteousness, rejected it for 120 years, and sealed their judgment.

Fourth, the hope of entrance into spiritual rest is based upon the authoritative Word of God (4:8). Although Israel entered Canaan under Joshua (the Old Testament equivalent for the name "Jesus"), they did not experience the total rest of God. If they had, then God would not "afterward have spoken of another day." They possessed the rest of Canaan, the place of physical blessing. After the conquests of the inhabitants, Joshua wrote, "And the Lord gave unto Israel all the land which he sware to give unto their fathers; and they possessed it, and dwelt therein. And the LORD gave them rest round about. . ." (Josh. 21:43–44).

B. The Exhortation to Labor (4:9–11)

The warning now concludes with a second admonition. Between the first ("let us fear") and the second ("let us labor"), the concept of rest is expounded.

1. The reality of rest (4:9–10)

There are three different words used for "rest" in the Scrip-tures. The first (*anapausis*) refers to the rest of sleep, the rest which brings positive refreshment to a weary person (Matt. 11:29; 26:45; I Cor. 16:18; Rev. 4:8). This first word does not appear in Hebrews.

The second (*katapausis*) occurs often in this book and was discussed earlier. It stresses cessation from activity, the quitting of work.

The third word (*sabbatismos*) is distinctively biblical, whereas the meanings of the first two were based upon the average work day of the natural man. This term underscores the sabbath rest of God and is used only once in the New Testament (4:9).

There are two principles of encouragement found in these two verses. First, there is a promise of rest available to each believer (4:9). The inferential conjunction "therefore" (*ara*) draws this conclusion from the preceding section where the psalmist spoke of a future rest. The usage of the present tense ("there remaineth") shows that the rest does not refer to heaven or to an experience after death; rather, it points out what a child of God can have right now. The rest also should not be equated with the gaining of initial salvation, because the promise is to those who are already "the people of God." The concept of rest (*sabbatismos*) is derived from the seventh day of the week of creation wherein God rested on the final day (Gen. 1:1—2:4).

Second, there is a position of rest which a believer can enjoy today (4:10). In fact, some had already entered ("he that is entered").[3] The rest of God ("his rest") refers to the cessation of activity. God worked for six days, then He stopped. On the seventh day, He superintended what He had done, but He no longer created anything new. Entrance into the rest of God thus means that a believer has "ceased from his own works, as God did from his."[4] Salvation is not gained by religious works, but by faith in the redemptive work of Christ (Rom. 4:5; Eph. 2:8-9).

3. Note the past tense. The verbal form is an aorist active participle (*ho eiselthōn*).

4. The verb "ceased" (*katepausen*) is the same word as "rest" (*katapausin*).

The abundant life is also acquired by faith, by resting in the divine provision, not by sight or by self-righteous works. At Kadesh, Israel looked at the obstacles of giants and walled cities, viewed only their own limited capabilities, disobeyed, and consequently failed to enter that place of divine provision for this life. Israel trusted God for their past deliverance, but would not trust God with the present or future. Both life and the abundant life are contingent upon faith, from beginning to end.

2. The appeal for rest (4:11)

The conjunction "therefore" (oun) introduces the conclusion to the third warning. Both the author and the readers are addressed in the exhortation ("let us labor"). It is better translated "let us strive earnestly," "let us give diligence," or "let us give haste" (spoudasōmen).[5] It stresses urgency, attentiveness, and quickness in decision making.

The warning of possible failure is contained in the negative result clause: "lest any man fall after the same example of unbelief." That example was Israel at Kadesh. The author did not want to have one single defector. Falling is the opposite of standing or advancing. To fall as Israel fell was to lose out on the gracious provisions of God for this life through lack of faith. There is no indication of loss of salvation.

II. THE WORD OF GOD (4:12-13)

Who or what can determine whether a person has genuine faith? The explanatory conjunction ("for") gives the answer and thus joins this passage to the preceding one. Only God can make that type of judgment, and He does it through the objective standard of His Word.

---

5. Aorist active subjunctive.

A. Its Qualities (4:12)

The phrase, "the word of God," can refer to the Lord Jesus Christ (John 1:1), the spoken word of God which has never been recorded, or to the spoken word of God which has been written by the prophets and the apostles. Since His spoken word has already been identified with the written canon (3:7; 4:4), the third possibility is the most plausible interpretation in this passage.

Five characteristics of the divine Word are enumerated in this verse.

1. Living

The Word is "quick" or, "living" (zōn).[6] It is living because the God who spoke it is living (3:12). God Himself gave this commentary on His Word:

> For as the rain cometh down, and the snow from heaven, and returneth not thither, but watereth the earth, and maketh it bring forth and bud, that it may give seed to the sower, and bread to the eater:
> So shall my word be that goeth forth out of my mouth: it shall not return unto me void, but it shall accomplish that which I please, and it shall prosper in the thing whereto I sent it (Isa. 55:10–11).

In the conclusion to the sermon on the Bread of Life, Christ claimed: ". . .the words that I speak unto you, they are spirit, and they are life" (John 6:63). In the parables the Word of God is often equated with seed which contains innate life, able to germinate and produce fruit (Matt. 13:19). God's Word can make a dead sinner alive through faith (Eph. 2:1).

2. Powerful

The adjective "powerful" can be transliterated as "energetic" (energēs). It literally means an "in working" or "work within." There is a moral, spiritual dynamic in the divine Word which can produce a transformation of character within a person.

---

6. Present active participle of zaō. It is very emphatic as a predicate adjective because it occurs first in the sentence.

Using the same word, Paul said that he served God "according to his working, which worketh in me mightily" (Col. 1:29). The Word not only tells men what to do, but it also provides the motivation and power to do it.

3. Sharp

The Bible is also "sharper than any twoedged sword." The sword mentioned here (*machairan*) was a small sword used in hand-to-hand combat. Another word (*rhomphaia*) is used for the sword which came out of the mouth of Christ in the symbolic vision of Him (Rev. 1:16; 2:12; 19:15). The latter refers to the lengthy blade. Paul equated the Word of God with the sword (*machaira*) of the Spirit (Eph. 6:17). This word was used of the weapons which the arresting soldiers possessed when they seized Christ at Gethsemane (Matt. 26:47), of the sword which Peter used to cut off the ear of Malchus (John 18:10), of the implement employed to kill the apostle James (Acts 12:2), and of the sword of the Philippian jailor (Acts 16:27).

The Word of God, however, is sharper than any sword which men can manufacture. The sword of man can only harm the body, whereas the sword of God can destroy both the body and the soul. It is incisive, distinguishing between the saved and the unsaved, the genuine and the false. The symbolism of the two edges may suggest the two testaments of the one Bible, the temporal and eternal qualities of the Word, or its application to both the saved and the lost. The Word, of course, is the basis of both divine salvation and judgment (II Cor. 2:15-16). Christ said: "He that rejecteth me, and receiveth not my words, hath one that judgeth him: the word that I have spoken, the same shall judge him in the last day" (John 12:48). A sword is an implement of defense and punishment. In the context of this warning, it becomes the means of divine chastisement for the erring believer and the standard of judgment for the unsaved.

4. Piercing

The Word of God can penetrate and discriminate in realms totally inaccessible to the natural man. It is "piercing even to the dividing asunder of soul and spirit, and of the joints and marrow." The first couplet refers to the psychological and immaterial constitution of man, and the second points to the physical and visible frame of the human being.

Evangelical theologians have debated the issue of the human essence for centuries. The question revolves around the parts into which a man can be divided. The position of trichotomy teaches that man has three basic parts: body, soul, and spirit. In this view the soul and the spirit are seen as two distinct entities (I Thess. 5:23). On the other hand, the adherents of dichotomy believe that man can be divided into only two parts: body and soul/spirit. To them, the soul and the spirit are accepted as synonymous terms or as titles for two different functions of the same immaterial part. All Evangelicals agree that man is both physical and immaterial in his basic constitution and that this physical–psychological life is passed directly from parents to their children. The disagreement arises over the essence of the immaterial part. Can it be further divided? The point of this passage is that only God through His Word can make the proper distinction. God thus knows things about a man which that man can not discern for himself.

5. Discerner

The Word is also a "discerner of the thoughts and intents of the heart." It is literally a "critic" (*kritikos*). The heart does not refer to the physical organ which pumps the blood. Rather, it describes the inner self of man, the ego. God knows what a man is thinking ("thoughts") and why he is thinking it ("intents"). He evaluates both the objective and the subjective aspects of the thought process.

B. Its Ministry (4:13)

1. Negative

God knows everything about all men and all things. Nothing escapes His omniscience or omnipresence. Every creature is "manifest" (*aphanēs*). He knows men inside out. The psalmist aptly confessed:

> O LORD, thou hast searched me, and known me.
>
> Thou knowest my downsitting and mine uprising, thou understandest my thought afar off.
>
> Thou compassest my path and my lying down, and art acquainted with all my ways.
>
> For there is not a word in my tongue, but, lo, O LORD thou knowest it altogether.
>
> Thou hast beset me behind and before, and laid thine hand upon me.
>
> Such knowledge is too wonderful for me; it is high, I cannot attain unto it (Ps. 139:1–6).

The psalmist further testified that he could never escape the presence of God, either in heaven or in hell (Ps. 139:7–12). He admitted that God perceived him even in his prenatal life (Ps. 139:13–16).

2. Positive

When men refuse to see themselves as they really are, God must remove their façade of pride and hypocrisy. The term "naked" (*gumna*)[7] points to the bare essence of a person. The church at Laodicea thought that it was "rich and increased with goods," but in reality, it was just "naked" (Rev. 3:17). The religious opponents of Christ claimed that they were the children of God and of Abraham, but Jesus asserted that they were really the children of the devil (John 8:39–44).

The verbal adjective "opened" (*tetrachēlismena*) is related to the Greek word for "neck" (*trachēlos*).[8] The verbal form was applied to an ancient wrestler who put a neck grip on his opponent. It was used of the gladiator who would put a sword

---

7. *Gymnastics* is based upon this Greek word.
8. The surgical operation of tracheotomy comes from this term.

under the chin of his adversary, lift up the head, and expose the neck to the spectators. It was also employed in the rite of pagan animal sacrifice when the priest slit the throat of the victim.

Men are rebels, determined to resist God. They are, however, extremely vulnerable to Him. They are subject to His judgment. They need to cry out for mercy.

III. THE PRIESTHOOD OF CHRIST (4:14-16)

At first glance there may not appear to be any connection between the warning drawn from Israel's past and the priesthood of Christ, but there are some specific transitional concepts. The conjunction ("then") forces the reader to search for the correlation. Actually, there are three key words in this passage which were mentioned earlier: the high priesthood of Christ (2:17; 3:1); the profession of the believer (3:1); and the boldness or confidence of the Christian (4:16; cf. 3:6).[9]

The priesthood of Christ, briefly mentioned earlier (2:17; 3:1), will now become the dominant theme of the remaining part of the book. In this section the relationship of the believer to Him is built upon two exhortations: "let us hold fast" (4:14) and "let us . . . come" (4:16).

A. Hold Fast (4:14-15)

Because they had forsaken the temple ritual, Jewish believers were often criticized for having no high priest (Acts 21:28). The present, continuous possession of Christ as a priest is empha-sized here by the double mention of "have" (4:14, 15). Two reasons are then given to encourage the child of God to continue his steadfastness.

9. The adverb "boldly" literally reads "with confidence" (*meta parrēsias*), the same word found in 3:6.

81

1. The position of Christ (4:14)

Three features can be seen. First, He is a "great high priest." In its history, Israel had many high priests. Some were godly and outstanding, but others were greedy and immoral. None, however, could compare with the greatness of Christ, in both His person (1:1—4:13) and His sacrificial work (4:14—10:18).

Second, Christ constantly functions as the priestly representative of the believer in the very presence of God. He "is passed into the heavens." There are three heavens mentioned in the Scripture: the atmospheric heaven that surrounds the earth (Deut. 11:11); the second heaven that contains the sun, moon, and stars (Gen. 1:14); and the third heaven, equated with paradise or the very presence of the Father (Isa. 63:15; II Cor. 12:2-4). After His death and resurrection, Christ ascended into the third heaven by literally "passing through" (dieleluthota) the other two (cf. 1:3; Eph. 4:10). In the scheme of the tabernacle and the temple, there were three areas: the outer court, the Holy Place, and the Holy of Holies. The high priest went into the third area, the Holy of Holies, only once per year on the Day of Atonement. He went in, sprinkled the blood on the mercy seat, and came back out. Christ, on the other hand, went into the heavenly Holy of Holies, the third section of the heavenly sanctuary, and has remained there. As the representative of His people, He can simply do more for them because He is there before God every day of every year.

Third, His name is "Jesus the Son of God." The first designation ("Jesus") stresses His humanity, whereas the second looks at His deity. He is one person with two natures. He thus understands both the position of man and the purpose of God. He is the perfect mediator between God and man because He is both divine and human (I Tim. 2:5). No Jewish high priest ever possessed that unique dimension.

2. The compassion of Christ (4:15)

The explanatory conjunction ("for") gives the second reason for the readers to hold fast to their profession of faith. Three evaluations of His compassionate ministry are given. First, Christ is "touched with the feeling of our infirmities." The phrase ("touched with the feeling") is the translation of one Greek infinitive (*sumpathēsai*), which literally means "to suffer along with." The English word "sympathy" is the transliteration of this term. The scope of "infirmities" goes beyond the physical problems of disease and death. It extends into the complex environs of the moral, spiritual, psychological, emotional, and social. In His earthly ministry, Christ manifested His compas-sion over the needs of men constantly: their lack of guidance, the grief of a widow, the despair of a father, and the mental aberration of a demoniac (Matt. 8:17). Jesus cared. He suffered along with those whose lives bore the effects of sin within the human race. On earth He delivered many of them from their problems.

Second, Christ was tempted as men are tempted. It is not sinful to be tempted, but it is sinful to yield to temptation. Since Christ gained a human nature at His incarnation, He became temptable. God, in His basic essence, cannot be tempted (James 1:13). It was within the will of God for Jesus to be tempted by Satan (Matt. 4:1-11). He was tempted "in all points." These "points" refer to the three major categories of temptation: the lust of the flesh, the lust of the eyes, and the pride of life (I John 2:16). Satan successfully used them to effect the fall of the first human pair (Gen. 3:6), but he failed in his attempt to get Jesus to disobey the will of God.

Third, Christ remained sinless in His life and ministry. He was "without sin." He had no sin nature, but He also did not think or do sin. Elsewhere it is written that He "knew no sin" (II Cor. 5:21), "did no sin" (I Peter 2:22), and "in him is no sin" (I John 3:5). Only Christ, among men, could challenge His critics: "Which of you convinceth me of sin?" (John 8:46). As human, Christ could be tempted, but as divine, He could not respond. He can sympathize with men in their infirmities but not in their sins.

B. Come (4:16)

In the profession of faith, a person must actively accept the deity of Christ. This commitment could produce an erroneous reluctance to voice one's needs to Him. The believer could question whether Christ really understands his human predicament or whether He would be interested in the problems of just one ordinary person. There was, therefore, a need to encourage believers to use the resources of Christ's compassionate priesthood.

1. The throne of grace

There was no throne of grace within the Jewish sacrificial system. Since Christ finished His redemptive work and sat down beside the heavenly throne, that throne has become a place where grace reigns and is dispensed. It has become the center of divine giving. The means of access to that throne has been made available to every believer; thus each can come "boldly," or "with confidence" (*meta parrēsias*). The emphasis of this phrase is upon the freedom to speak, to voice one's needs with the full knowledge that requests in the will of God will be granted. Esther and Mordecai wondered about what might happen if she approached the king without being invited (Esth. 4:11), but the believer should have no such fears as he comes into the presence of his heavenly Father.

2. Mercy

The concept of "mercy" contains the idea of divine pity. God is "plenteous in mercy" (Ps. 103:8). He pities them that fear Him (Ps. 103:13). A believer needs forgiveness and the removal of the natural consequences of his sins and errors. He can obtain such mercy from His gracious Father.

3. Grace

The believer can also find "grace to help in time of need." The "time of need" is literally a "good time" (*eukairon*). A needy believer wants divine assistance at the right time.

Questions for Discussion

1. What does it mean to fear God? To fear man?

2. Can distinctions be made between false professors and genuine believers who disobey? If so, what are they?

3. Does this passage speak to the issue of the time period of creation? Were the days ages or regular calendar days?

4. How can a believer learn to trust God more in his life? How is faith increased?

5. What is the difference between unbelief in the life of a Christian and that within an unsaved person? Are there any similarities?

6. How does the Word of God evaluate us? Give examples.

7. Relate your tests and temptations to those of Christ. What are the similarities? Differences?

5

The Two Priesthoods
Hebrews 5:1-14

The exposition of the priesthood of Christ continues in this chapter as it is contrasted with the priestly order established under the Mosaic Law. In the total comparison between the two, the author demonstrates that Christ has a better position, namely in the third heaven (4:14-16); that He belongs to the better order of Melchizedek (5:1-7:28); that He functions under a better covenant, the new covenant with its better promises (8:1-13); that He serves in a better sanctuary (9:1-11); and that He offered a better sacrifice (9:12—10:18).

The conjunction ("for") forms the transition from the last chapter to this one. The believer should hold fast his profession and should come to the heavenly throne of grace because he has a High Priest who is totally qualified. A priest had to be human and divinely appointed (5:1-4), and Christ was both (5:5-10).

I. THE TWO ORDERS (5:1-10)

This passage introduces two more important Old Testament personages: Aaron (5:4) and Melchizedek (5:6, 10). Both are vital in that they functioned as high priests and started orders of priesthood which were named after them. Melchizedek ministered before the giving of the Mosaic Law whereas Aaron served after its introduction to Israel.

A. The Order of Aaron (5:1-4)

From the creation of Adam to the exodus of Israel out of Egypt, the male head of the family had the responsibility to offer sacrifices unto God (Gen. 9:20; 12:8; Job 1:5). After the Exodus, God sanctified the firstborn males of each family for priestly service (Exod. 13:2). When Israel made the golden calf and then worshiped it, God selected the tribe of Levi to take the place of the firstborn males (Exod. 32:15-28; Num. 8:5-26). Concerning the relationship of the Levitical tribe to Aaron, God charged that He had "given the Levites as a gift to Aaron and to his sons from among the children of Israel, to do the service of the children of Israel in the tabernacle of the congregation" (Num. 8:19). The tribe of Levi was itself divided into three parts: the sons of Gershon, who cared for the tent and the curtains; the sons of Kohath, who watched over the tabernacle furniture; and the sons of Merari, who were responsible for the hardware (Num. 3:17, 25-37). The actual priesthood centered in Aaron and his sons (Num. 3:10). A priest within Israel, therefore, had to prove his genealogical descent to Aaron and the tribe of Levi. If he could not do so, then he forfeited his right to serve (Neh. 7:63-65).

1. The qualifications (5:1a)

No Jewish high priest was exempt from these qualifications. The principle focuses on each specific example, not just on the general order (note "every"). The common feature of these qualifications is the humanity of the priest. Three aspects are given. First, he must be "taken from among men." No angel nor any other nonhuman creature could fit the position. Even God, in the full essence of His deity alone, could not qualify. The high priest had to be a human being, and he had to be selected from the members of Aaron's family. Concerning the first high priest of Israel, God instructed Moses, "And take thou unto thee Aaron thy brother, and his sons with him, from among the children of Israel, that he may minister unto me in the priest's office" (Exod. 28:1). God also charged Moses to separate the Levites in the same way (Num. 8:5-6).

Second, the priest must represent other men and serve their interests. He thus "is ordained for men." He is their vicar, or substitute. There is no self-appointment to this task; he must be ordained by God.

Third, the high priest must represent men before God. His ministry centered "in things pertaining to God." He did not function as a mediator between men nor as God's emissary to men. His service centered in that which was spiritual, ritualistic, and moral. His life revolved around the tabernacle (or the temple that replaced the tabernacle), the religious calendar, and the complex sacrificial system. His destiny was not to be a prophet, a king, a businessman, or a farmer. In fact, when the land of Canaan was divided among the tribes, the tribe of Levi received no portion. They were to live in cities within the various tribal allotment. The God of Israel was "their inheritance" (Josh. 13:33).

2. The ministry 5:1b–3)

The conjunction ("that") introduces three purposes of the high priest's ministry. The first purpose was to offer sacrifices for the people (5:1b). The verb "may offer" (*prospherēi*) literally means "to bring before." He had a never-ending activity of bringing before God the offerings of the Israelites.[1] The objects of bringing are listed in two general categories: "gifts" (*dōra*) and "sacrifices" (*thusias*). This distinction is seen twice more in the book (8:3; 9:9). There were five major offerings in the ritualistic system: burnt, meal, peace, sin, and trespass (Lev. 1–7). The contrast between the gifts and the sacrifices may possibly be seen in the sweet savor offerings (burnt, meal, peace) and the nonsweet savor offerings (sin, trespass). The former were voluntary, whereas the latter were obligatory. Another possible difference may be that the gifts were nonbloody offerings (grain and wine) and the sacrifices were bloody, requiring the death of the victims (animals and birds). The cause for the offering was the "sins" (*hamartiōn*) of the people. These sins were defined as

1. Indicated by the present tense of the verb.

the actual violations of the Mosaic Law in its moral, civil, and ceremonial applications. All sin is ultimately a lack of conformity to the character and will of God, but these sins would also embrace intentional and unintentional wrongs against both the person and the property of a neighbor (Lev. 16:16).

The second purpose of the high priest's ministry was to have compassion on the people (5:2). Since the high priest was human, he had an innate and filial ability to manifest his feelings toward the offenders. The verb "have compassion" (*metriopathein*) is unique, literally meaning "to suffer a little or moderately."[2] He had to maintain a position of balance between the extreme of apathy ("no suffering") and excessive feeling and excitement. He had to perform his vocation according to the prescribed laws, but he could not be cold or merely professional. He could not condone the sins of the people, but his heart had to reach out to them. Justice had to be tempered by love and tenderness. The object of his compassion was literally one group of people: "the ones who were ignorant and wandering astray" (*tois agnoousi kai planōmenois*).[3] The source of their sins was ignorance, and the result was a deviation from the Mosaic Law. Ignorance of the law was no excuse for its violation, but God did distinguish between sins of ignorance and those which were committed presumptuously (Num. 15:24–31). There was no sacrifice prescribed for the latter sins, and such offenders were punished with physical death. Even the sin of stealing had to be examined on the basis of motivation. There was a difference between thievery for personal gain and that for the elimination of hunger (Prov. 6:30–31). The cause of the compassion was the priest's own "infirmity," or better, "weakness" (*astheneian*). He was encompassed or clothed with the same moral dilemma as the people he represented. He recognized the natural tendency of men to err because he himself had failed many times. He knew about the sins of omission and commission from personal experience. He shared in their human depravity. He knew what

2. Used only here in the New Testament.
3. Note the usage of one article followed by two verbal adjectives. This is an illustration of the Granvile Sharp rule of grammar. The KJV suggests that the objects were two separate groups.

God wanted him to do, but he was also aware of the fact that in himself he had no moral power to do it.

The third purpose of the high priest's ministry was to offer sacrifices for his own personal sins (5:3). In the original instructions for the Day of Atonement Aaron had to wash his body before he offered "his bullock of the sin-offering, which is for himself, and make an atonement for himself, and for his house" (Lev. 16:6). After he did that, he washed himself again and then offered a burnt offering to make an atonement "for himself, and for the people" (Lev. 16:24). In this procedure he dealt with himself first, then he identified himself with the people in their national sacrifice (9:7). At all times in the performance of his elevated ministry, he had to be aware of his own moral insufficiency. In human essence he was just like everyone else.

3. The call (5:4)

The high priesthood of Israel, of course, carried with it much honor. Because of that fact, two foundational principles were incorporated into the Mosaic Law. The first, expressed negatively, was that "no man taketh this honor unto himself." The average Israelite could not aspire to this position. He could not train for it, buy it, or seize it by force. Self-appointment was impossible. Within the church a male can seek the office of a pastor if he meets the character qualifications (I Tim. 3:1–7). The most godly man within Israel, however, could not hope to become the high priest.

The second, expressed positively, is that the high priest had to be "called of God." Divine selection, preparation, and appointment were absolutely necessary. This was the method by which the first high priest of Israel, namely Aaron, was called.

The initial indication of the divine selection of Aaron can be seen at the time Moses expressed his shyness and poor public speaking ability to God. God then assigned Aaron to be the official spokesman for Moses before the people (Exod. 4:10–18). Later Moses charged Aaron to lay up a pot of manna before the Lord (Exod. 16:33). At Sinai God charged Moses to separate

Aaron and the latter's sons and to confirm their divine appointment into the office of priest (Exod. 28:1). Subsequently during
the wilderness wanderings a protest against the leadership of
Moses and Aaron was led by Korah, Dathan, and Abiram,
members of the tribes of Levi and Reuben (Num. 16:1). These
three and their followers were then supernaturally killed when
an earthquake swallowed them up as they dared to intrude into
the tabernacle with the strange fire of priestly incense (Num.
16:28–35).

Further divine confirmation of the exclusive appointment of
Aaron came when twelve rods or dry sticks engraved with
twelve tribal names were placed in the tabernacle. The name of
Aaron was written on the rod assigned to the tribe of Levi. God
then made this pronouncement: "And it shall come to pass, that
the man's rod, whom I shall choose, shall blossom: and I will
make to cease from me the murmurings of the children of
Israel. . ." (Num. 17:5). Only Aaron's rod budded, bloomed, and
brought forth almonds (Num. 17:8). That rod was then kept
within the ark of the covenant in the Most Holy Place of the
tabernacle as a continuing testimony to the divine call of Aaron
and his sons.

B. The Order of Melchizedek (5:5–10)

At this juncture in the argument of the book, the author did
not undertake a technical contrast between the priestly orders
of Aaron and Melchizedek. Rather, the qualifications of Christ
to be a priest for all mankind are given. It will be demonstrated
that He is human, compassionate, and divinely called.

1. The appointment of Christ (5:5–6)

The transitional words ("so also") show the fulfillment of the
previous requirement (5:4). First, Christ "glorified not himself to
be made an high priest." He did not take that prized honor unto
Himself (5:4). Christ did not appoint Himself. He was not selfishly
ambitious in His ministry, either through His preaching or His

crucifixion. Christ's total preoccupation was in complete obedience to the will of God (10:7). He Himself testified, ". . .I seek not mine own will, but the will of the Father which hath sent me" (John 5:30). He came in His Father's name (John 5:43). Christ knew that the restoration of His eternal glory would occur after the completion of His earthly task (John 17:4–5), but He did not glorify the Father just to regain His own glorification. He earlier confessed, "If I honour myself, my honour is nothing: it is my Father that honoureth me. . ." (John 8:54). The glorification of the Father by Him meant that the Father would be glorified in the Son. The intrapersonal relationship of the Father to the Son consequently produced a reciprocal glorification of the two divine persons, but at no time did Christ seek His own glorification.

Second, Christ received divine appointment to the office of High Priest (5:5b–6). This fact is proved by two verbal statements made by the Father to the Son. Both are contained in quotations lifted from two Davidic psalms. The first, mentioned earlier (1:5; Ps. 2:7), stresses the human nature of the divine Son, which He obtained at His incarnation through the virgin conception and birth. The Father begat the Son in the sense that He brought the eternal Son into human existence through the ministry of the Holy Spirit in the body of Mary. If this quotation has more particular reference to the resurrection, as some assert, then it is the resurrection of the divine–human Christ. He could not have a resurrection unless He was first totally human.

The second quotation (5:6; Ps. 110:4) states the actual divine appointment of Christ to the priesthood: "Thou art a priest for ever after the order of Melchisedec." Melchizedek is mentioned only twice in the Old Testament (Gen. 14:17–24; Ps. 110:4). He was both a king and a priest. He was the king of Salem (probably Jerusalem) and also "the priest of the most high God" (Gen. 14:18). He met Abraham after the latter rescued Lot. Melchizedek blessed the father of the Jewish people, and Abraham in turn gave tithes to him. Under the Mosaic system, Christ could not become a priest because He was born into the kingly tribe of Judah, not the priestly tribe of Levi. The order of Melchizedek, however, predated the order of Aaron. In the later messianic psalm of David, it was further established that the priesthood of the Messiah would be according to the order of Melchizedek. The Messiah of Israel thus was to be both a king and a priest. The Dead Sea sect believed in the advents of two messianic figures: a king from the line of David and a priest from the family of Aaron. Their confusion stemmed from their ignorance of the importance of Melchizedek. The actual priestly ministry of Aaron ended with his death and his order terminated with the destruction of the second temple (A.D. 70), but Christ's priesthood goes on forever because He has been raised from the dead and lives forever in the presence of the Father (7:24–25).

2. *The learning of Christ (5:7–8)*

The main focus of this section is upon the fact that Christ was both human and humane. The emotional qualities of His inner self and His compassionate identification with others can be viewed from His experience in Gethsemane and at the cross. Through those events, He "learned" (5:8). The omniscient God, in the essence of His deity, never has learned, and yet Christ did.

Four aspects of that learning process can be detected from these verses. First, He learned "in the days of his flesh." This phrase denotes the period from His incarnation through the virgin conception to His death and resurrection. The eternal Son of God was made flesh (John 1:14). The mystery of the redemptive plan is the truth that "God was manifest in the flesh" (I Tim. 3:16). Earlier the author stated that Christ partook of flesh and blood (2:14). The phrase thus points out His earthly, human existence and has nothing to do with a fleshly, sinful nature (Rom. 8:3). Learning is a natural quality of humanity. Since Christ obtained a perfect human nature through Mary, He went through the normal process of learning as men learn. From His birth to the age of twelve, Jesus "grew, and waxed strong in spirit, filled with wisdom" (Luke 2:40). From the age of twelve to thirty, He "increased in wisdom and stature, and in favor with God and man" (Luke 2:52).

Second, Jesus learned through His prayers in Gethsemane.

Jesus Christ was a man of prayer. He was praying when the Holy Spirit descended on Him shortly after His baptism (Luke 3:21). He often withdrew into the wilderness to pray (Luke 5:16). He prayed all night before He selected the twelve apostles (Luke 6:12–13). His transfiguration occurred as He was praying (Luke 9:29). Such prayers, for both self and others, naturally manifested His dependence upon the Father and revealed His identification with the human race. On the night before His crucifixion, Jesus showed His intense compassion for sinful men through His agonizing prayers in the Garden of Gethsemane (Matt. 26:36–46). At that time He offered up "prayers and supplications." The first word (*deēseis*) stresses the idea of intense entreaty, even to the point of begging. Its urgency can be seen by its use in the requests of the leper (Luke 5:12), the demoniac (Luke 8:28, 38), the father of a possessed child (Luke 9:38, 40), and the distressed Simon (Acts 8:24). Such prayer marked the disciples (Acts 4:31), Cornelius (Acts 10:1–2), Paul (Rom. 1:10), Zacharias (Luke 1:13), Anna (Luke 2:37), and the disciples of John the Baptist (Luke 5:33). Such prayers bring response from God (I Peter 3:12). The second term (*hiketērias*) focuses on the need of protection and help in the midst of calamity.[4]

The actual content of the prayers and supplications was accompanied "with strong crying and tears." The former refers to loud, vocal outbursts whereas the latter underscores the intense emotional strain. Christ definitely experienced physical and psychological suffering then. In fact, His agony was so severe that He sweat "as it were great drops of blood" (Luke 22:44).

His prayers were directed toward the Father, the one who "was able to save him from death." What was the essence of this death? Various views have been suggested. Some believe that Christ wanted to be delivered from a premature physical death in the Garden. Others contend that He desired to be saved out of the realm of physical death through the resurrection; however, He claimed that He had the power of self-resurrection (John 10:18) and that He had come to die on the cross (John 12:27).

4. Used only here in the New Testament.

The most plausible position is that He prayed to be delivered from the realm of eternal death, the second death of separation from God. The punishment for sin is both physical and spiritual death (Rom. 6:23). At the cross Christ experienced this double death in order to provide both physical and spiritual redemption for lost humanity. A priest could show compassion because he himself had sinned in the same ways. Christ, however, showed His compassion by His total awareness of what would happen to Him when the sin of the entire world was placed upon His sinless self.

His prayers were heard and answered in that He was restored to fellowship with God after being judicially forsaken by Him and was raised from the tomb. He "feared" in that He had an acute concern for the honor of a holy God. He thrice acknowledged that He wanted to do God's will (Matt. 26:39, 42, 44).

Third, He learned in spite of the fact that He was divine. Even though He was the only one who could rightly call Himself "Son" (1:2, 5), He was willing to become sin for a lost world (II Cor. 5:21).

Fourth, He learned the total essence of obedience through His sufferings on the cross. Gethsemane anticipated them, and Golgotha fulfilled them. Paul wrote that Christ "became obedient unto death, even the death of the cross" (Phil. 2:8). This sacrifice of self was the ultimate expression of humiliation. The nature of obedience is total submission to the will of another. His obedience made possible divine justification, whereas the disobedience of Adam produced universal condemnation (Rom. 5:18–19). The means of obedience was "by the things which he suffered." The physical suffering came from man, but the spiritual originated with God. He "was stricken, smitten of God, and afflicted" (Isa. 53:4).

3. The saviorhood of Christ (5:9–10)

Through His incarnate human experience Christ "became" (*egeneto*) that which He was not before. He became "the author" (*aitios*)[5] of the divine redemptive program. Three characteristics

5. Used only here in the New Testament. It is related to the word for "cause" (*aitia*).

of His divine–human saviorhood can be seen in these two verses. First, its basis was in His perfection. The participle "being made perfect" (*teleiōtheis*)[6] stresses the completion of a process. In the life of Christ, it was achieved at the cross when He used the same verb in His triumphant exclamation: "It is finished" (*tetelestai;* John 19:30). The perfection of the Redeemer and the redemption were finalized at the same time. In the anticipation of His death, Christ could say that He had finished the divine work for His life (John 17:4). The saviorhood process began at the Incarnation and continued through His human development; His ministry, which was rejected by Israel; His agony in Gethsemane; and His passion on the cross.

Second, its result was the giving "of eternal salvation unto all them that obey him." The provision of salvation was achieved through the obedience of the Son to the Father at the cross, and the appropriation of salvation is accomplished through the obedience of the repentant sinner toward Christ. In this passage, obedience is synonymous with faith (Acts 6:7; Rom. 6:17; 10:16). The obedience involves compliance with His prescribed regulations for salvation (John 5:24). It does not view salvation as a reward for works of righteousness (Rom. 4:5; Eph. 2:8–9). The nature of the verb indicates that man bears the responsibility for either the acceptance or rejection of Christ.[7]

Third, recognition of Christ's human–divine saviorhood is seen in the official, divine salutation of His eternal priesthood (5:10). The decree to establish Christ in the order of Melchizedek occurred in the eternal counsel of God, but the public acknowledgment of the fulfillment of that decree occurred after the Crucifixion and Resurrection. The verbal form "called" (*prosagoreutheis*)[8] means "to salute or address." It is a compound word which literally means "before the marketplace." It thus denotes the most public notification which could be orally expressed. God thus gave formal recognition to the priestly person and work of Christ upon the latter's ascension into heaven.

6. Aorist passive participle.
7. Present active participle.
8. Used only here in the New Testament.

II. THE IMMATURITY OF THE READERS (5:11-14)

There is now a transition from an objective evaluation of the priesthood of Christ to a subjective analysis of the spiritual condition of the readers. The prepositional phrase ("of whom") refers to Christ in His priestly relationship to Melchizedek. The author now confesses that the complexities of that relationship may be too difficult for his readers to comprehend. He concludes that they are spiritually immature.

A. Marks of Immaturity (5:11-13)

There is a difference between maturity and spirituality and between immaturity and carnality. Maturity involves time, growth, and experience, whereas spirituality stresses a believer's momentary relationship to the Holy Spirit. A believer who is walking in the Spirit is spiritual because he wants to be controlled by Him, but that same Christian may be immature if he has just been saved for a short time (Gal. 5:16). A carnal child of God is one who responds to a problem out of his sinful human nature (I Cor. 3:3-4). Believers in their practice and disposition can thus possess these characteristics in pairs. The goal of each saint should be maturity and spirituality. The worst position would be immaturity and carnality. He could however be mature and carnal or immature and spiritual. The readers were basically immature with periodic lapses into carnality.

1. Limited capacity (5:11)

The learning process involves both the teacher and the student. First, the author, as the teacher, had a double problem. He had "many things to say" about the priestly ministry of Christ. There was much content and little time in which to communicate it (13:22). The task to condense the material thus became difficult. The selection of words and their syntactical relationships became critical. Another problem facing him was the explanation of the material. It was "hard to be uttered" (*dusermēneutos*), or literally "hard to be interpreted."[9] People often read but do not perceive biblical truth. All truth, no matter how simple, still needs to be exegeted, and therein was the problem of the author.

Second, the readers as the students were "dull of hearing." The adjective "dull" (*nōthroi*) comes from two words: *ne* ("not") and *otheō* ("to push"). A dull person, therefore, has no push or drive; he is slow or sluggish. The readers were dull in the realm of hearing. They seemed to have no desire to hear new instruction. The verb "are" (*gegonate*) is better translated, "you have become and are now."[10] They had become dull by personal choice. They were once alert to the voice of God, but their persistent doubts caused them to become restricted in their capacity to receive truth.

2. Lack of growth (5:12)

Life should issue in growth. The analogy of the physical life shows that a believer should advance from immature babyhood to mature adulthood (I Peter 2:2). The readers had failed in their growth process. Three observations are given. First, they had been saved a long time (10:32). For their chronological years in the faith, they should have become the "teachers" of others. They had enough time in which to graduate from spiritual grammar school, junior high, senior high, and college.

Second, the readers still had a need to understand the foundational truth of the Christian faith. In a sense, they were still in spiritual "first grade." The "oracles of God" doubtless refer to the Old Testament and to those New Testament books with which they were familiar (Acts 7:38; Rom. 3:2; I Peter 4:11). The "first principles" (*stoicheia*) dealt with the redemptive plan of God as it was progressively revealed: the lost condition of man; the inability of man to keep the moral law of God; the purpose of the Jewish sacrificial system; and the provision of salvation through the work of Christ who fulfilled the Old Testament types and prophecies.

9. The science of hermeneutics, which deals with the principles of biblical interpretation, is based upon this Greek word.

10. Perfect active indicative.

Third, they retrogressed in their spiritual diet. They had "become such as have need of milk, and not of strong meat." An exclusive milk diet is satisfactory for newborn infants, but it is an alarming practice for adults. Their apathy had not only hindered their progress, but it also produced retrogression. Hewitt astutely observed, "If the dark things do not become plain, then the plain things will become dark."[11] The "milk" refers to the first principles of the Christian faith (5:12; 6:1-2), whereas the "strong meat" points to advanced doctrinal truth and its application to the issues of life. The sense behind "strong meat" is that of "solid nourishment" (*stereas trophēs*).

3. Lack of skill (5:13)

A babe lacks the ability to make sound decisions. He is not able to integrate doctrine with duty. The adjective "unskillful" (*apeiros*) literally means "no test." He thus has no successful experience in the application of Scripture to problem solving in moral and personal situations. A spiritual babe must be told what to do and how to do it, but a mature Christian can make those decisions for himself.

B. Marks of Maturity (5:14)

In the real world, the path from immaturity to maturity varies with each individual, but the end result is the same. Some children are forced to grow up faster because they had to make adult decisions in their youth.

1. Unrestricted diet

Mature believers are they "that are full age" (*teleiōn*), the ones who have attained the goal of spiritual perfection. Since they have advanced into adulthood, the time when they can teach

11. Thomas Hewitt, *The Epistle to the Hebrews* (Grand Rapids: Eerdmans, 1981), p. 101.

others from their knowledge of the Scripture and from their own experience, they can enjoy the blessing of strong meat. The Holy Spirit can guide them into all sections of the Scripture, and they are able to assimilate it into their framework of doctrine and practice.

2. Responsible decisions

A mature Christian has the capacity to make intelligent decisions ("by reason of use"). He recognizes the mistakes of his past, but he has the good sense to learn from them. He knows what to do and what to avoid. He has a proper sense of timing. He appreciates the relevance of the written word of God to his contemporary culture.

In addition, a mature Christian has an acute sensitivity for a godly lifestyle ("have their senses exercised"). He has a cultivated sense of caution in the presence of moral danger whether it be explicit or implicit.

A mature Christian can discern between "good and evil." These adjectives do not refer to the vast difference between the moral absolute of goodness (agathos) and wickedness (poneros). Rather, he can distinguish between the good results (kalos) and the bad results (kakos) of a decision which has not yet been made.

Questions for Discussion

1. Should Christian leaders discuss their own failures or their feelings with their people?

2. How can believers have more compassion for others? How can it be manifested properly?

3. Does God call men into the ministry today? What is the essence of the divine call?

4. What qualities of humanity can be seen in the prayer life of Christ? Is dependency an admission of human weakness?

5. Why do Christians retrogress into immaturity? How can they be stimulated to advance?

6. What is milk doctrine? Meat? What is the diet of most believers?

7. How does maturity grow out of decision making? Give some illustrations.

6

The Appeal for Progress
Hebrews 6:1-20

Immaturity and indecision go together. A lack of confidence in God breeds instability and spiritual hesitation. The children of Israel manifested these weaknesses at Kadesh-barnea. They paused there and sent in spies because they did not trust God's promise that the land was theirs for the taking.

This chapter will contain an urgent appeal for the readers to progress toward their divinely appointed goals (6:1-3), a warning about possible failure (6:4-8), an encouragement concerning their spiritual condition (6:9-12), and a reminder of divine integrity (6:13-20).

I. THE FOURTH WARNING (6:1-12)

The inferential conjunction ("therefore") joins the warning to the preceding discussion of the readers' immaturity. Their spiritual hesitation could lead to an irreversible catastrophe comparable to that which Israel experienced in the wilderness at Kadesh-barnea. The author, alarmed over this possibility, recognized that the only solution was in a concerted move toward maturity prompted by faith in God.

A. Exhortation (6:1-3)

1. Its goal (6:1a)

The author again addressed himself as well as his readers in his command: "Let us go on." It is better translated, "Let us be borne along," or "Let us be carried forward (*pherōmetha*)."[1] The essence of the verb is a common willingness to be lifted up by God and to be carried toward spiritual victory. In such compliance, there can be no resistance, but there must be a constant determination to be moved forward by the Spirit.

The goal is "perfection" (*teleiotēta*). Just as Christ achieved perfection through the completion of His divinely appointed tasks (5:9), so a believer should strive toward the "end" (*telous;* 6:11) God has purposed for him. The perfect end for Israel was the enjoyment of divine provision within Canaan, but most of the people forfeited that blessing through their immature unbelief. The goal of perfection for the child of God is a conformity to the moral nature of God (Matt. 5:48) and a performance of the revealed purpose of redemption (Phil. 3:12-15). This perfection can be seen in spiritual maturity penetrated by the controlling presence of the Holy Spirit. In essence, it is all that is enveloped within the abundant life promised by the Savior (John 10:10). In fact, it is the Christ life in its total expression (Phil. 1:21).

2. Its requirements (6:1b-2)

In general, two actions had to be taken before progress could occur. First, the person must leave "the principles of the doctrine of Christ." The sense behind "leaving" (*aphentes*) is separation. It denotes neither repudiation nor deprecation. It implies rather the passing from one phase of contemplation to another. For example, a student of calculus does not reject the basics of elementary mathematics when he is concentrating on his more difficult subject. The above phrase literally reads, "the word of the beginning of Christ," a synonymous expression for "the first principles of the oracles of God" (5:12).

1. Present passive subjunctive.

Second, the believer must not lay again the foundation of his Christian life. In construction no builder places a foundation upon another. Once the foundation is in place, it is necessary to go forward with the erection of the structure (I Cor. 3:10–11). Hughes believes that the foundation is "characteristic of the evangelistic preaching and practice of the apostles as recounted in the book of Acts."[2] Others have suggested that the foundation refers not to the basic theological truths of the Christian faith as expounded in the epistles, but rather to the Old Testament prophecies which found their fulfillment in the earthly ministry of Christ. It is impossible to ascertain with absolute certainty the total scope of the mentioned foundation. All must recognize, however, the obvious transitional period covered by the Gospels and the Book of Acts in which there is a movement from Judaism to Christianity, from Israel to the church.

The foundation is listed in six specific areas. They can be grouped together as pairs under three categories pertaining to salvation (6:1b), initial church experience (6:2a), and future things (6:2b). The first area is "repentance from dead works." These are the works of the Mosaic Law by which no person could be justified (Gal. 2:16; 3:11–12). They were dead in that they were incapable of producing eternal, spiritual life. Both Jesus and John the Baptist preached a gospel of repentance (Matt. 4:17; Mark 1:15). They called people to change their minds about their relationship to God and their confidence in the rites of the sacrificial system. Genuine repentance, however, does issue in living works (Matt. 3:8; Acts 26:20). Such works are the evidence of salvation, not its cause. In order to mature, a believer must settle conclusively that legalistic conformity has no merit before a holy God, either before or after regeneration. There thus would be no value for a Jewish believer to cling to his allegiance to the temple, the priesthood, or the ritual calendar.

The second area is "faith toward God." Repentance is nega-tive, whereas faith is positive. The former involves rejection, but the latter stresses acceptance. Paul charged men to "repent and turn to God" (Acts 26:20). When genuine faith occurs, trust is

2. P. E. Hughes, *A Commentary on the Epistle to the Hebrews,* (Grand Rapids: Eerdmans, 1977), p. 196.

turned from self-confidence to the redemptive nature of God. The value of faith lies in the one upon whom it is placed.

The third area is the "doctrine of baptism" (*baptismōn didachēs*). The usage of the plural embraces the various types of baptisms with their functions and meanings. The Jewish legalistic system incorporated "divers washings," or baptisms (9:10; same word). Christ criticized the Pharisees for their vain commandments and traditions, including the baptism, or "the washing of pots and cups" (Mark 7:8; same word). Within Judaism, there were ceremonial purifications by water and the practice of proselyte baptism (John 3:25). John the Baptist proclaimed the baptism of repentance whereby a convert showed his faith in the imminence of the coming of the Messiah and His kingdom (Luke 3:3). The disciples of Jesus also baptized in the anticipation of His kingdom (John 3:22-23; 4:1-2). The previous two baptisms both presupposed the remission of sins through repentant faith. Jesus was baptized by John to show His identification with the believing remnant, to manifest His messiahship to Israel, and to be the occasion for His anointing by the Holy Spirit (Matt. 3:13-17; John 1:26-34). The symbolism behind Christian baptism is a public identification with Christ in His death and resurrection (Matt. 28:18-20). In addition, the baptism in the Holy Spirit is the means by which a believer is placed into the body of Christ, the true church (I Cor. 12:13).

The fourth area is the "laying on of hands." The Mosaic Law stipulated that a person should "put his hand upon the head of the burnt offering," namely the animal of sacrifice (Lev. 1:4). On the Day of Atonement, the high priest placed both of his hands on the goat which was then sent into the wilderness (Lev. 16:21). At that time the priest confessed over the animal "all the iniquities of the children of Israel, and all their transgressions in all their sins" (Lev. 16:21). Christ placed His hands on children when He blessed them (Matt. 19:13). On some occasions He also laid His hands on the infirmed when He healed them (Mark 7:32-33). The apostles laid their hands on seven men, signifying their approval and appointment of the seven to the diaconate (Acts 6:6). The selection of elders involved the laying on of hands (I Tim. 4:14; 5:22). The Samaritan converts received the Holy

Spirit when Peter and John placed hands on them (Acts 8:17). The action of laying on of hands thus symbolized recognition, identification, and approval.

The fifth area is the "resurrection of the dead." The Old Testament taught this doctrine (Job 19:25; Isa. 26:19; Dan. 12:2). The genuine Jewish believer knew that he would be raised from the dead in the last day (John 11:24). Christ taught that He would raise both the saved and the lost in two separate resurrections (John 5:28-29). There was confusion, of course, over the relationship of the death and resurrection of the Messiah to Israel, the church, and the masses of lost humanity. His resurrection consequently became the guarantee of the resurrection of all others (I Cor. 15:20-25). Deliverance from the physical penalty of death via resurrection was an integral part of the gospel message (I Cor. 15:1-4).

The sixth area is "eternal judgment." The psalmist declared that the ungodly would not be able to escape divine judgment (Ps. 1:5-6). For the unsaved, judgment inevitably follows physical death (9:27). Christ announced that all who lacked faith in Him would face condemnation (John 5:24). The foundation involving judgment probably involved a discussion of sheol or hades, gehenna or the lake of fire, and the great white throne (Rev. 20:11-15).

3. Its possibility (6:3)

The achievement of the goal is possible if the will of a believer and the will of God agree. The author fully expected that his readers and he would continue to advance toward perfection ("and this we will do"). He however fully acknowledged that God must allow it to happen ("if God permit"). It is always the moral will of God for a believer to mature and to develop a life of holiness. It is also within the sovereign will that a believer may die, even apart from divine chastisement, before he realizes his aspirations for this life. Both Paul and James admitted that future plans should always be made in total subjection to divine permission (I Cor. 16:7; James 4:13-15).

B. Warning (6:4–6)

The explanatory conjunction ("for") gives the reason behind the exhortation. A warning for deliberate disobedience is given. The verbal, grammatical flow of this section can be seen in these concepts: "Let us go on . . . for it is impossible . . . to renew them again unto repentance."

1. Objects of the warning (6:4–6a)

There is great debate over the spiritual condition of the objects of this warning. Are they saved or unsaved people?[3] There is an observable change from the first person pronoun ("we" and "us"; 6:1, 3) to the third person ("they" and "them"; 6:4, 6). Hewitt argues, "The change of pronoun . . . suggests that these pronouns are different from the readers."[4] Actually, the third person pronouns do not appear in the Greek text of this passage, but they serve as the translation for the articular participle (tous phōtisthentas, literally "the having been enlightened ones"). This switch indicates that the author wanted to present the warning in an impersonal, objective fashion rather than in a direct appeal as used before (2:3; 3:8, 12). He later admitted that the readers had not yet succumbed to the perilous, irreversible situation (6:9).

The spiritual position of the objects of the warning must be concluded from the meaning of five participles used to describe them.[5] First, they were "once enlightened" (tous hapax phōtisthentas). Some of the early church fathers equated this phrase with the rite of baptism. It actually refers to the event of regeneration when a sinner, dominated by moral death and darkness, passes into spiritual life and enlightenment. At that transforming experience, God "shined in our hearts, to give the light of the knowledge of the glory of God in the face of Jesus Christ" (II Cor. 4:6). Using the same word, Paul charged that the

3. This author believes that they were saved.
4. Thomas Hewitt, *The Epistle to the Hebrews* (Grand Rapids: Eerdmans, 1981), p. 106.
5. One article appears with the entire series of participles. According to the Granville Sharp rule of grammar, they are descriptive of just one group.

eyes of understanding were enlightened at conversion (Eph. 1:18). In fact, the author later used the same verbal concept to describe the readers' entrance into the family of God: "But call to remembrance the former days, in which, after ye were illuminated [*phōtisthentes*]. . ." (10:32). The addition of the adverb ("once") stresses the complete, once-for-all act of divine illumination upon the blinded mind of the unregenerate.

Second, they "tasted of the heavenly gift." Some of the early church fathers identified this phrase with the rite of the Eucharist. Those who claim that these verbal phrases describe unsaved professors believe that sinners can taste without fully assimilating the benefits of salvation. This same term, however, was used of Christ when He tasted death for every man (2:9). He did not sample death; rather He experienced death in all of its totality. Peter stated that newborn babes in the Christian faith are those who "have tasted [same word] that the Lord is gracious" (I Peter 2:3). The imagery of tasting and eating is based upon the declaration of the psalmist: "O taste and see that the LORD is good: blessed is the man that trusteth in him" (Ps. 34:8). In His sermon on the Bread of Life, Christ equated the reception of eternal life by faith with the eating of His flesh (John 6:51–58). Salvation is a "gift," not the reward for meritorious deeds of religious and humanitarian service (Eph. 2:8–9). The gift is "heavenly" in that its source is from heaven and its essence is both eternal and divine, not earthly and temporary.

Third, they "were made partakers of the Holy Spirit" (*metochous genēthentas pneumatos hagiou*). The same concept of partaking is used elsewhere of the readers sharing in the heavenly calling (3:1), in Christ (3:14), and in the divine chastisement of the children of God (12:8). The Spirit of God does restrain sin within the human race (Gen. 6:3; II Thess. 2:6–7). He also reproves the world of sin, righteousness, and judgment (John 16:8). The unregenerate thus do share in His ministry, but they do not partake of Him. There are only two groups of people in the world today: the saved who have the Holy Spirit dwelling within them and the unsaved who do not have the Spirit (Rom. 8:9). The verbal form looks back to the time when they came to be in the Spirit and He in them. This spiritual union is the seal of the redemptive purpose, the guarantee of eternal life (I Cor. 6:19; II Cor. 1:22; Eph. 1:13; 4:30).

Fourth, they "tasted the good word of God and the powers of the world to come." In regeneration a person is saved "not of corruptible seed, but of incorruptible, by the word of God which liveth and abideth for ever" (I Peter 1:23). The content and direction of saving faith comes through the Scriptures (Rom. 10:17). Christ equated the eating of the heavenly Bread with the internal reception of His words, which bore the essence of spirit and life (John 6:63). The term "powers" (*dunameis*) was used earlier of the "divers miracles" which God demonstrated in the authentication of the ministries of Christ and the apostles (2:4). In this passage, however, it refers to that divine power and glory which will be evident in the age to come, the millennial kingdom which will epitomize the fulfillment of the new covenant made by the shed blood of Christ (Jer. 31:31–34; Luke 22:20). The knowledge of God and the moral transformation of the believer into Christlikeness are contemporary indicators of what life will be like when Christ returns to the earth (II Cor. 3:18).

Fifth, they had fallen away. The English conditional clause ("if they shall fall away") is actually a translation of one Greek participle (*parapesontas*).[6] The translators of the King James Version and many commentators believed that the verbal form was a conditional participle used in an adverbial fashion.[7] However, the usage of the connective ("and"; *kai*) before the participle shows that it is part of the series of five participles. All have an attributive function in the total description of the group under discussion. The sense of the warning must be taken in this way: It is impossible to renew again to repentance the people who have been enlightened and have tasted and have become partakers and have fallen away. All of the verbal adjectives point out events that had been completed in their past.[8] The reason

6. This verb is used only here in the New Testament. It is an aorist active participle.

7. H. E. Dana and J. R. Mantey, *A Manual Grammar of the Greek New Testament* (New York: Macmillan, 1957), p. 227.

8. They are all aorist participles.

STAND BOLD IN GRACE

for the omission of the second person ("you") and first person ("we") pronouns from this theological dilemma is the fact that neither the author nor the readers had fallen away, even though the other four verbal adjectives described their true spiritual condition. If the other two pronouns had been used, there would have been no need for the warning since they would have been beyond the point of rescue.

How can a believer fall away? At Kadesh-barnea, Israel fell away when they refused to enter Canaan in faithful obedience to the command of God. It was impossible to renew that unbelieving generation to repentance the day after their critical decision even though some of them wanted to enter. In like manner, a believer can manifest his distrust in the leadership of God at a crossroads decision in his life. He has fallen away to a point wherein he can never reverse the consequences of his resolution. He doubtless committed the type of sin which leads to severe divine chastisement, even a premature physical death (John 15:6; I Cor. 11:30; James 5:19-20; I John 5:16).

2. Extent of the warning (6:6b)

Concerning the fallen individuals, the author dogmatically declared that it was "impossible . . . to renew them again to repentance." There is a repentance which is essential to salvation (Mark 1:15; Acts 2:38; II Peter 3:9). There is also a repentance for a sinning Christian, fostered by a godly sorrow, which can restore him to divine blessing and fellowship (II Cor. 7:9-10). A believer, however, can lose the possibility of repentance through deliberate disobedience. Saul forfeited for himself and his posterity the possibility of kingly rule over Israel when he dared to officiate as a priest (I Sam. 13:13-14). Esau lost any future opportunity of spiritual leadership when he sold his birthright to Jacob (12:16-17). In fact, he "found no place of repentance, though he sought it carefully with tears" (12:17). Israel could not go into Canaan once they refused to do so at Kadesh-barnea. Even though people may change their minds after they recognize the consequences of their deeds, God forbids them from recovering their lost opportunities.

At Kadesh, Israel repudiated the redemptive nature of God. They openly confessed that the God who brought them out of Egypt could not take them into Canaan. They questioned His integrity and goodness. It was a public disavowal before the pagan nations. In like manner, a believer can bring public embarrassment to the person and redemptive work of Christ by a refusal to go on to maturity and to the provisions of the abundant life. In that sense, he publicly discredits what Christ has done for him and what He wanted to do in his life. Such people thus "crucify to themselves the Son of God afresh, and put him to an open shame."

3. Meaning of the warning

Here are some of the major views in the interpretation of this warning. First, the objects were professing Christians who really did not possess salvation. The Scofield Reference Edition of the Bible states that they were "Jewish professed believers who halt short of faith in Christ after advancing to the very threshold of salvation."[9] In this view Canaan is equated with salvation and Kadesh with the point of individual decision. However, Israel had already escaped the bondage of slavery in Egypt. The only unpardonable sin for a sinner is to state that Christ performed His miracles by Satan rather than by the Holy Spirit (Matt. 12:22–32). The opportunity to repent for salvation is open to the unsaved right up to the point of their physical death.

A second view says that they were saved people who lost their salvation through their fall. If that view were correct, then this passage would also teach that such a person could not regain his salvation a second time. The clear teaching of Scripture is that salvation is a gift from God maintained by His faithfulness, not conditioned upon man's works (John 10:27–29; Rom. 8:28–29; Eph 2:8–9).

Third, the passage contains a hypothetical situation which actually could not happen in real life. The main criticism of this view is that it removes the value of the warning.

9. P. 1295.

Fourth, it is impossible for a person to become saved, to be lost through falling, and then to be saved again. Advocates state that if that situation were possible, then the second event of salvation would remove the judgment of the moral and doctrinal lapse. The warning thus would lose its practical effectiveness. This view has much plausibility and appears to suit the context.

Fifth, a believer can forfeit future earthly blessings through a critical decision of falling away.[10] He can fail to achieve the intended purpose for his life. God cannot renew him or bring him into his personal Canaan because he has disqualified himself from that possibility.

C. Illustration (6:7-8)

An illustration from nature and agriculture is given to show the contrast between obedience and disobedience in the life of a believer.

1. Fruitfulness (6:7)

The "earth" represents the child of God, and the "rain" symbolizes the provision of God necessary for a life of productivity. The purpose of the earth is to "bring forth herbs" and the goal for the believer is to manifest "fruit unto holiness" (Rom. 6:22) and to achieve "perfection" or spiritual maturity (6:1). By abiding in Christ through moral purity and submission to Him, a Christian can produce the fruit of Christlikeness (John 15:1-6). The production of fruit may vary from one saint to another, but it will be there (Matt. 13:23). Just as farmers expect to receive crops from that which they have planted, so a believer should produce a godly life for God and His glory ("for them by whom it is dressed"). The obedient Christian thus will receive "blessing from God." In earthly life, this blessing includes answered prayer, the inner satisfaction of the glorification of God, the experience of total discipleship, the warmth of divine love, and genuine joy (John 15:7-11). At the judgment seat of Christ, the

10. Author's view.

obedient Christian will receive divine commendation and eternal rewards (I Cor. 3:12–14).

2. Fruitlessness (6:8)

The fallen Christian is likened to earth "which beareth thorns and briers." These manifest carnality, the works of the flesh (Gal. 5:16–17). This person fails to achieve the divinely intended purpose for his life. Three results of this failure are listed. First, he is "rejected" (*adokimos*). The adjective literally means "unapproved." The term, translated as "reprobate," is used of the unsaved several times (e.g., Rom. 1:28; II Tim. 3:8; Titus 1:16). Paul, however, mentioned the possibility that he could become a "castaway" (I Cor. 9:27; same word) if he did not discipline his life in morally pure service for God. The procedure of divine testing upon a believer can bring either approval or disapproval (I Thess. 2:4).

Second, the fallen Christian is "nigh unto cursing." The believer has been redeemed from the curse of the law (Gal. 3:10, 13). He cannot return to the cursed position of the unsaved (II Peter 2:14), but he can approach that place where he can be judged for his sins in this life. That experience is comparable to the divine punishment of the unsaved on this earth (Rev. 18:4–5).

Third, the fallen Christian's "end is to be burned." Although this might appear to be a reference to hades or to the lake of fire, it really points to the judgment seat of Christ where a fruitless, wasted life will be examined by fire (John 15:6; I Cor. 3:13). Just as the thorns of the earth are burned, so the carnal works of a Christian will be consumed to show that they had no eternal value. The true end of a Christian should be fruitful, spiritual maturity, but many construct their own self-destructive ends.

D. Assurance (6:9–12)

In his conclusion, the author assessed the spiritual condition and motivation of his readers, He expressed confidence that they would go on to perfection and that they would not fall.

1. Of their salvation (6:9)

The address ("beloved") indicates the readers' possession of salvation (I John 4:1). The author then expressed his firm conviction of their salvation ("we are persuaded").[11] He knew that they would produce "better things," namely "herbs" rather than "thorns and briers." He expected them to manifest the "things that accompany salvation." In order for that to take place, they must have salvation within them.

2. Of divine remembrance (6:10)

All faithful work done for the glory of God will be rewarded by Him. That biblical axiom is based upon the righteous nature of God ("For God is not unrighteous to forget"). That fact further substantiates the possession and the permanence of their salvation. If a saved person could lose his salvation and end up in hell, how could God reward him for the righteous works which he committed after regeneration?

Five areas of commendation are given. First, the readers' "work" (*ergou*) was evident. This term stresses what they had done since they had been converted (Eph. 2:10).

Second, these believers had performed a "labor of love" (*tou kopou tēs agapēs*). This phrase stresses the strenuous effort put forth in the work (I Thess. 1:3; 2:9). Quantity is measured by the work and quality by the labor. Both were motivated by a genuine love for Christ and for their fellow believers (II Cor. 5:14; I John 3:14).

Third, these Christians "showed" their work and love toward the name of God. They did it for His honor and glory. Their purpose and motivation were theocentric, not autocentric. They had no ulterior goals.

Fourth, these believers had "ministered to the saints" in their postregeneration past. They had served others through hospitality and deeds of mercy.

11. Perfect tense.

114

Fifth, they were still engaged in benevolent service ("do minister").[12] They were still producing fruit, thus God and the author had not given up on them.

3. Of his desire (6:11-12)

The author then expressed a threefold desire for his readers. First, he wanted them to reach maturity (6:11). He was concerned about each individual as well as the entire group ("every one of you"). He wished that each would "show the same diligence," the same firm resolution of the inner spirit. He could not achieve the divine end for them; rather, they had to internalize his desire and to work hard for its fulfillment. Their effort, however, had to express "the full assurance of hope." Their decision to move on to maturity should reveal the firm conviction (*plērophorian*) of their heart. This term was used of Abraham's assurance that God would keep His promise and give him a son (Rom. 4:21). Their resolution could not be marked by doubt or hesitation. The "end" (*telous*) is "perfection" (*teleiote* 6:1), or maturity, the divine goal for each believer.

Second, the author did not want his readers to become permanently "slothful" (*nōthroi*). This term was translated earlier as "dull" (5:11). He desired them to be spiritually alert, teachable, and sensitive to divine direction.

Third, the author wanted his readers to follow the example of successful, godly men who exhibited "faith and patience" before they received the inheritance of the divine promise (6:12b). The term "followers" (*mimētai*) stresses imitation and is the basis of the English "mimic." Their present sin was doubt and anxiety.

II. THE EXAMPLE OF ABRAHAM (6:13-20)

There are many godly examples in Scripture, but Abraham, the father of the nation of Israel, is specifically isolated. Both

12. Note the change from the past to the present tense.

saved and unsaved Jews could consider him. He believed, endured, and inherited the promise of God to him.

A. The Promise of God (6:13–15)

1. Its statement (6:13–14)

The divine promise to the patriarch was stated in the Abrahamic covenant (Gen. 12:1–3, 7; 13:14–18; 15:18–21; 17:1–8). In it God promised to establish Abraham as the father of the great nation of Israel, to bless him, to make his name great, to cause him to bless others, to reward his friends and to judge his enemies, to bless the entire world through him, to give him and his physical posterity the land of Canaan, and to be his God. The promise especially centered in the future birth of a son to the childless patriarch and his barren wife, Sarah. In order to have a nation, they had to begin with one son.

The only guarantee of fulfillment was the unconditional word of a God of integrity. God was alone responsible for the statement of promise and for its accomplishment. He "sware by himself," because there was no person outside of His divine being who was greater (6:13). The promise embraced multiple and excessive blessing and physical descendants (6:14; Gen. 22:16–17). It was reiterated after the willingness of Abraham to sacrifice Isaac, the promised son (Gen. 22:1–14).

2. Its realization (6:15)

A span of twenty-five years elapsed between the initial giving of the Abrahamic covenant (Gen. 12:1–3) and the birth of Isaac (Gen. 21:1–5). In that period, the patriarch "patiently endured." He "against hope believed in hope, that he might become the father of many nations" (Rom. 4:18). He did not permit the weakness of his body or the deadness of Sarah's womb to dissuade him. He was strong in faith, confident that God would perform what He had promised (Rom. 4:19–21).

Abraham finally "obtained the promise" in the birth of Isaac.

Moses wrote, "And the Lord visited Sarah as he had said, and the Lord did unto Sarah as he had spoken" (Gen. 21:1). The reward of faith is the inheritance of divine promise.

B. The Oath of God (6:16–18)

God gave to Abraham not only His promise, but also His oath. The promise contains the content of the covenant, and the oath represents the unconditional guarantee of its fulfillment.

1. Its value (6:16)

In human situations men "swear by the greater" to reinforce the truthfulness of their word. The oath is designed "for confirmation" and as "end of all strife." It is both a guarantee of integrity and a solution to disputes. In most predicaments men appeal to higher authorities such as their parents, their religious leaders, or God. In contemporary courts men swear to tell the truth before God and man with the help of God.

2. Its permanence (6:17)

Hughes observed: "That God should bind himself by an oath is a reflection not on the divine credibility but on the perversion of the human situation. God's oath, indeed, though in itself is redundant since His word is absolute truth (John 17:17), is a condescension to human frailty."[13] God did accommodate Himself to the known procedures of man, even to "the heirs of promise." God will do whatever He wills to do, and what He wills composes His unconditional promise to His children. That truth reflects "the immutability of his counsel." His purpose cannot be frustrated; it will come to pass. Nevertheless, God confirmed His covenant promises to Abraham with an oath (Gen. 15:1–21).

13. Hughes, *A Commentary on . . . Hebrews,* p. 229.

3. Its encouragement (6:18)

God is truth, therefore He cannot lie. His promise and His oath thus are the "two immutable things" which men can trust at all times. Those two verities should produce "strong consola-tion" within those who must endure by faith. To escape the bondage and penalty of sin, believing sinners have "fled for refuge" to God, who has promised eternal life to all who call upon Jesus Christ. In that act of faith they came "to lay hold upon the hope" set before them. That hope is the assurance of life after death in a resurrected, glorified body. That hope involves eternal fellowship in the Holy City. Believers, through faith and patience, must wait for that fulfillment.

C. The Hope of God (6:19–20)

The relative pronoun ("which") connects this section with the preceding discussion and specifically with its grammatical ante-cedent, the "hope."

1. It is an anchor (6:19)

Five observations about the hope of God can be seen. First, the hope is the "anchor of the soul." The function of an anchor is to keep the ship from moving from a selected position. It is also unseen as it sits submerged on the ocean floor, and yet its influence tugs on the ship. The hope of eternal fellowship with God likewise can keep the soul of the believer from drifting from its divinely appointed purpose (2:1).

Second, the hope is a present possession of each Christian ("we have"). Paul wrote: "For we are saved by hope: but hope that is seen is not hope: for what a man seeth, why doth he yet hope for? But if we hope for that we see not, then do we with patience wait for it" (Rom. 8:24–25).

Third, the hope is "sure" (*asphalē*). This term stresses its indestructibility from outside sources. Nothing can separate the believer from the love of God (Rom. 8:35–39).

Fourth, the hope is "stedfast" (*bebaian*). This word refers to the inner strength of the anchor, the hope. It has no innate weak-nesses which will become evident in time.

Fifth, the hope is found in the very presence of God ("which entereth into that within the veil"). In this context, the veil is that which stood in the doorway into the Most Holy Place of the tabernacle or temple.

2. It is Christ (6:20)

The hope or anchor is Jesus Christ. His very presence before the Father is the guarantee of the divine promise and oath that the believer will also appear in heaven.

He is the "forerunner" (*prodromos*). This term was used of soldiers who were sent in advance of a marching army. No high priest within Israel was a forerunner because no Israelite fol-lowed him into the inner sanctuary. Christ, in the order of Melchizedek, went into the heavenly tabernacle and has re-mained. He has promised to return in order to take the saints into glory (2:10; John 14:1-3).

Questions for Discussion

1. What is involved in perfection? How can a Christian know when he has reached spiritual adulthood?

2. How knowledgeable about the fundamentals of the faith are believers? How can such understanding be examined?

3. What causes believers to fall away from spiritual advance-ment? How can this perilous situation be prevented?

4. How can a believer bring shame to Christ? To the local church? To himself?

5. How can believers become disapproved? How can this be prevented? Can such saints be recovered to fruitful service later?

6. What is involved in genuine repentance? For the saved? For the unsaved?

7. Are Christians impatient? How can they learn to endure by faith?

Christt, Melchizedek, and Levi
Hebrews 7:1–28

The contrast between the priestly orders of Melchizedek and Levi will be concluded in this chapter. Three major arguments will be seen: Melchizedek is positionally better than both Abraham and Levi (7:1–10); the prediction of a new priest of the order of Melchizedek shows the temporary character of the Levitical system (7:11–22); and the Levitical ministry ended at death, but the priestly service of Christ continues forever because He rose from the dead (7:23–28).

I. MELCHIZEDEK (7:1–10)

This important personage is mentioned in only three passages of Scripture (5:5–7:28; Gen. 14:17–24; Ps. 110:4). The conjunction ("for") links this discussion with the previous references to Melchizedek (5:6, 10; 6:20).

A. His Person (7:1–3)

1. His titles (7:1)

Melchizedek has two significant titles. First, he was a "king of Salem." Salem was an ancient name for Jerusalem, which is the equivalent of Mount Zion. The psalmist declared, "In Salem also is [God's] tabernacle, and his dwelling place in Zion" (Ps. 76:2).

Second, he was also a "priest of the most high God." The Hebrew text uses the phrase "El-Elyon" to support this translation (Gen. 14:18). As such, He is the "possessor of heaven and earth" because He created them (Gen. 1:1; 14:19, 22). The term "highest" (*tou hupsistou*) does not mean that there are many gods and that He is the greatest of them; no other god exists. The term depicts His unique supremacy over the created order. Elsewhere Christ is acknowledged as the Son of the Highest [same word] by the demons (Mark 5:7; Luke 8:28) and by Gabriel (Luke 1:32).

Melchizedek figures prominently in only one historical event of the Old Testament era. He met Abraham after the patriarch rescued the kidnapped Lot and killed the four kings responsible for the abduction (Gen. 14:1–24). At that time Melchizedek provided bread and wine and blessed the father of the Hebrew people with these words: "Blessed be Abram of the most high God, possessor of heaven and earth: And blessed be the most high God, which hath delivered thine enemies into thy hand" (Gen. 14:19–20).

2. His meaning (7:2)

At the historic meeting Abraham gave "a tenth part of all" the goods which had been retrieved from the conquered kings to Melchizedek (Gen. 14:11–12, 16, 20). The tithe was presented to God through His priestly representative.

At this point of the argument for the superiority of Melchizedek, the meanings of his name and position are put forth. The proper name "Melchisedec" is a Hebrew compound word composed of the words for "king" (*melek*) and "righteousness" (*zedek*).[1] The city name "Salem" means "peace" (cf. *Shalom*). He was a king whose person and realm were marked by righteousness and peace.

In like manner, Christ is the messianic king whose kingdom will manifest the righteousness of God and peace among men (Isa. 32:17). One of His titles is "The Lord Our Righteousness"

---

1. Hebrew words are built upon a series of three consonants. His name is thus based upon MLK and ZDK.

(Jer. 23:5-6). He is also "The Prince of Peace" (Isa. 9:6). Melchizedek thus typified the royalty of Jesus Christ.

3. His life (7:3)

Melchizedek appears and exits from the historical record with slight notice. Neither the name of his father ("without father") nor that of his mother ("without mother") is stated. No genealogy contains his name. The phrase "without descent" literally means "no genealogy" (*agenealogētos*). The Levites needed to prove their tribal heritage through the genealogical records in order to qualify for the priestly ministry (Ezra 2:62-63; Neh. 7:63-65). There is no record of Melchizedek's birth or death ("having neither beginning of days nor end of life").

The author concludes that these facts of silence cause Melchizedek to be "made like unto the Son of God." As God, Christ is eternal, with no beginning or ending. Some commentators have concluded that Melchizedek was actually a Christophany, an appearance of Christ in human form before His incarnation. However, it would be difficult to argue that He was a priest after the order of Himself. It is better to conclude that the typical significance of Melchizedek lies in the fact that he was both a king and a priest. Christ is the King, possessing the royal birthright of David out of the tribe of Judah, and is the Priest by divine oath. Levitical priests ministered for only twenty years, from the age of thirty to fifty (Num. 4:3, 22, 33). Melchizedek "abideth a priest continually" in that there is no record of the finish of his priestly service. Christ, with His eternal divine nature and resurrected human body, likewise has a never ending priesthood.

B. His Position (7:4-10)

The author now challenged his readers to "consider how great" Melchizedek was. The verb (*theōreite*) stresses constant contemplation with insight and discernment.[2] They needed to

2. Present active imperative.

recognize the historical facts and the theological deductions in them.

1. He is better than Abraham (7:4–7)

The historic meeting between these two key men produced two actions which support the assertion that Melchizedek is better than Abraham. The superiority is in position, not in person; it is functional, not ontological.

First, Abraham gave a tithe to Melchizedek (Gen. 14:20). This tenth part came out "of the spoils" (*ek tōn akrothiniōn*). This compound word, consisting of "top" (*akros*) and "heap" (*this*), literally means "the top of the pile," indicating the best of the spoils of victorious conquest.

The significance of this tithing procedure lies in the fact that there was no racial connection between the two men. Jacob, the grandson of Abraham through Isaac, had twelve sons including Levi. After the exodus of Israel from Egypt, God appointed the tribe or "the sons of Levi" to "the office of the priesthood" (7:5a; Exod. 32:26; Num. 3:5–13). They were originally designed to assist Aaron and his sons in the service of the tabernacle. The Levitical tribe itself was divided into three units based upon the three sons of Levi: Gershon, Kohath, and Merari (Num. 3:17). The Levites received from God "a commandment to take tithes of the people according to the law" (7:5b; cf. Num. 18:21). They had no inheritance in the land of Canaan after Joshua conquered it (Deut. 12:12; Josh. 13:33). They were to live in cities within the various tribal allotments and to be supported by the tithes of the other tribes, "their brethren" in the flesh. In turn, the Levites had to give a tithe to the family of Aaron (Num. 18:25–32). This brotherly support reinforced their common derivation from Abraham (7:5b).

Melchizedek, however, had no racial "descent" or genealogical connection with either Abraham or his physical descendants (7:6a), yet he received tithes from Abraham.

The second basis of superiority can be seen in the fact that Melchizedek blessed Abraham, the one who had received the covenant promises (7:6). The author then referred to a natural law of human relationships with which all would agree ("without all contradiction"). The principle, perceived either deductively or inductively, was clear and simple: ". . .the less is blessed of the better" (7:7). Based upon that presupposition, Melchizedek was thus better than Abraham, the father of the Hebrew nation.

2. He is better than Levi (7:8–10)

There are two lines of support for the above title statement. First, the reception of tithes by the Levites ended at their respective deaths, whereas no end of the ministry of Melchizedek is recorded (7:8). The contrast is further indicated by the adverbs: "here . . . there."[3]

Second, the superiority is further seen by the theological conclusion that Melchizedek blessed Levi and that Levi gave tithes to Melchizedek (7:9–10). The author, by the Spirit of God, then declared a biblical truth which could never be detected from the historical events or characters ("and as I may so say"). He charged that Levi "payed tithes in Abraham." The family descent of the patriarchs was: Abraham—Isaac—Jacob—Levi. Levi thus was the great-grandson of Abraham. When the historic encounter occurred, Abraham had no children at all, and he definitely died before Levi was born (Gen. 25:7–11). The author then answered this obvious rhetorical question: How could Levi pay tithes to Melchizedek when he was not yet alive?

The answer is couched in a theological mystery, a truth which could only be known through divine revelation and illumination: Levi was seminally present in Abraham. The writer states: Levi "was yet in the loins of his father [Abraham], when Melchisedec met him." Levi did not begin to exist as a person until his own conception by Jacob and Leah (Gen. 29:34). However, life passes from one generation to another. The genetic and physical–psychical constitution of a living human being is de-

3. The usage of "here" shows that the book was written while the second temple was still functioning before A.D. 70.

rived from his parents back to grandparents and ultimately back to the first human pair, Adam and Eve. The Scriptures teach of other seminal identifications with past ancestors. The entire human race sinned in Adam and shared in his judgment of death (Rom. 5:12). Christ was seminally present in His physical ancestors through Mary when Israel came out of Egypt (Matt. 2:15; Hos. 11:1). Through regeneration, a believing sinner participates with Christ in His crucifixion and resurrection (Gal. 2:20). This spiritual union of oneness assures the believer of total acceptance before God. The regenerated mind of a Christian, therefore, must accept by faith the paradox that Levi was present in Abraham. Since Melchizedek received tithes from Abraham and blessed the patriarch, the king–priest consequently received tithes from Levi and blessed Levi. Melchizedek is better than Levi because the less is blessed by the better (7:7).

II. LEVI (7:11–22)

The sacrificial system of the Jerusalem temple was based upon the Mosaic Law and the Levitical priesthood. The priesthood of Christ, after the order of Melchizedek, was not related to either one of them. In this section the author argues that God proposed a change from one system to another.

A. Prediction of Change (7:11–17)

The stimulus in this passage is the concept of "perfection" (*teleiōsis;* 7:11). The readers had already been urged to go on unto "perfection" (*teleiotēta;* 6:1) or the "full age" of spiritual maturity (*teleiōn;* 5:14). The question was over the method of accomplishment: the Levitical system of priests, sacrifices, rituals, and legalistic conformity to the Mosaic Law or the access of grace through faith in the person and redemptive work of Jesus Christ. How could the divine purpose for each regenerated individual be attained?

1. The new order (7:11-12)

Four theological and exegetical conclusions can be derived from these verses. First, God never intended that perfection would come by the Levitical priesthood, which encompasses all aspects of the ceremonial regulations: sacrifices, diet, religious calendar, and place of worship (7:11a). The protasis actually states a contrary to fact condition ("If therefore perfection were by the Levitical priesthood").[4] It could neither remove sin nor give righteousness. It could provide neither justification, sanctification, nor glorification.

Second, there is an inseparable connection between the Levitical priesthood and the entire Mosaic Law with its moral, civil, and ceremonial implications. Under the priesthood, the people of Israel "received the law" (7:11b). The law was a unit given to Israel at Sinai. The nation accepted it with these words: "All that the LORD hath spoken we will do" (Exod. 19:8). They did not differentiate between the sacrifices and the Ten Commandments. Both came from God and deserved their obedience under the watchful guidance of the priestly system.

Third, the prediction of the advent of another priest according to the order of Melchizedek shows that the Levitical system was temporary and incomplete (7:11c). Again the author used the messianic psalm of David to prove his point (Ps. 110:1, 4). The adjective "another" (heteron) means one of a different kind. If spiritual growth for the believer could have been realized through the legalistic system, then God would never have announced the coming of a new priest out of an order which preceded that of Levi and Aaron.

Fourth, the replacement of the Levitical order of priesthood necessitated "a change also of the law." Since the law and the priesthood were an integral part of each other, the removal of the one also meant the removal of the other (7:12). The dispensation of the Mosaic Law served its purpose in the divine plan for Israel, but its supervision of the lives of people ended at the cross with the death of Christ (Gal. 3:19-25; Col. 2:14-17). John put

4. It is indicated by the usage of ei ("if") with a secondary verbal tense "were" (ēn).

126

the change into stark contrast: "For the law was given by Moses, but grace and truth came by Jesus Christ" (John 1:17). Early Jewish believers were often criticized for their refusal to follow the old legalistic regulations of Jewish life (Acts 6:14; 21:20).

2. The new priest (7:13–17)

Jesus Christ is "he of whom these things are spoken" (7:13a). Two facts about Him are set forth. First, He is a physical member of the tribe of Judah. Jewish priests came from the tribe of Levi, but Christ descended from "another tribe, of which no man gave attendance at the altar" (7:13b). When Saul, who was of the tribe of Benjamin, intruded into the office of the priest by offering a sacrifice, he forfeited his kingdom to David (I Sam. 13:8–13). The prophet Samuel rebuked him: "Thou hast done foolishly: thou hast not kept the commandment of the LORD thy God, which he commanded thee" (I Sam. 13:13). When Uzziah, the king of Judah, went into the Solomonic temple to burn incense, God punished him by afflicting him with leprosy (II Chron. 26:16–21). At that time, Azariah the priest resisted him: "It appertaineth not unto thee, Uzziah, to burn incense unto the LORD, but to the priests the sons of Aaron . . ." (II Chron. 26:18).

The evidence of biblical history and genealogical ancestry shows that "our Lord sprang out of Judah" (7:14). Judah was the tribe which produced the rightful kings of Israel. On his death bed, Jacob pronounced blessings upon his twelve sons (Gen. 49). He declared that the right to rule would rest within Judah (Gen. 49:8–12). God subsequently gave this promise to David who was of Judah: "And thine house and thy kingdom shall be established for ever before thee: thy throne shall be established for ever" (II Sam. 7:16). That covenant promise was repeated by the angel Gabriel to Mary who also was of the family of David (Luke 1:30–33). Luke recorded the physical ancestry of Jesus through Mary (Luke 3:23–38).[5] In it he traces Christ back to David, Judah,

5. The author accepts the position that Luke's genealogy is that of Mary whereas that recorded by Matthew (chap. 1) is of Joseph. For a detailed discussion of the genealogies, see the author's book *The Virgin Birth: Doctrine of Deity* (Grand Rapids: Baker, 1981), chap. 17.

Abraham, and Adam. Paul declared that Christ "was made of the seed of David according to the flesh" (Rom. 1:3; cf II Tim. 2:8). Christ was born in the city of David, namely Bethlehem of Judah (Mic. 5:2; Luke 2:4, 11).

Second, Christ is a priest after the order of Melchizedek (7:15–17). The evidence of the Davidic, messianic psalm (Ps. 110) definitely anticipated the advent of a new king–priest (7:15). No ordinary Jew could meet that qualification because he could not be born out of two different tribes, namely the priestly tribe of Levi and the royal tribe of Judah. Israel thus was caught in a paradoxical dilemma: How could her Messiah–Redeemer be both a king and a priest and how could He be both divine and human?

Christ gained His royal right through His physical ancestry, but His priesthood is not based upon any human genealogy. The Jewish priests became such "after the law of a carnal commandment" (7:16a). It was "carnal" (sarkikēs) in that it pertained to human birthrights in the flesh. The genetic circumstances of their births dictated whether their personal future would be involved in the priesthood. On the other hand, Christ gained His priesthood by His death and resurrection ("after the power of an endless life"). The event of physical death terminated the priestly ministry of the Levites, but it actually began His service. He continues His priestly ministry in a glorified, resurrected, and ascended body. Whereas Jewish priests became such because their human fathers were priests, Christ became a priest by the oath of God (7:17).

B. Fact of Change (7:18–22)

1. The commandment is set aside (7:18)

The redemptive work of Christ effected the "disannulling of the commandment." The term "disannulling" (athetēsis) is later used of the putting away of sin by Christ (9:26).[6] It thus means to abolish or to render inoperative. The verbal form (atheteō) can

---

6. The noun is found only twice in the New Testament, both times in Hebrews.

be seen in the rejection of the divine law by the traditions of men (Mark 7:9), the despising of Christ (Luke 10:16), the repudiation of the spiritually proud by God (I Cor. 1:19), and the despising of the Mosaic Law (10:28). The sacrifice of Christ ended the era of the Levitical order and the animal offerings.

There were two major problems with the law even though it was divinely given and intrinsically holy, just, and good (Rom. 7:12). It possessed "weakness" (*asthenes*) in that it could not eliminate the *cause* of man's sinful position before God. It revealed to man the holiness of God and the depravity of the human race. It could not produce justification because the source of a right standing before God lay outside of itself and because of man's inability to obey (Rom. 8:3). The commandment was also "unprofitable" (*anōpheles*) in that it could not remove the effects of sin. It had no innate power to produce change within a sinner. It could tell the unregenerate what to do, but it could not enable him to do it. The law thus could neither begin nor end the process of spiritual perfection (7:19a).

2. The new hope brings perfection (7:19)

The failure of the law involves also the failure of the Levitical order. It could not produce justification or sanctification; it "made nothing perfect" (*eteleiōsen*). Paul argued that God never intended for the law to give righteousness and eternal life to the unsaved who were dead in their sins (Gal. 3:21). The law, however, was designed to bring man to a sense of moral guilt and to direct him to put his faith in God for salvation (Gal. 3:22–24).

The "better hope" centers in the divine–human person of Jesus Christ and in His redemptive crucifixion and resurrection. Christ conquered both the cause and effects of human sin at the cross; and through His resurrection, He is free to empower every believing sinner for a holy life. The presence of Christ in the believer is "the hope of glory" (Col. 1:27). By his identification with Christ in His death and resurrection, the believer can live for God because Christ is living in him (Gal. 2:20). He thus is guaranteed ultimate glorification (Rom. 8:28–30). The believer through Christ thus has unrestricted access into the very presence of God ("by the which we draw nigh unto God").

3. The new covenant is sure (7:20–22)

Two principles are stated. First, the oath of God guarantees the immutability of Christ's priesthood (7:20–21). He did not become a priest "without an oath" (7:20). The Levitical priests did not need a divine oath to receive their ministry (7:21a). They were born into the priesthood established under the Mosaic covenant. The priesthood of Christ, however, was established both positively ("sware") and negatively ("will not repent") by God. The first verbal action is the unconditional declaration, whereas the second stresses the eternal permanence of the decree. There is no possibility of change in the priesthood of Christ, but the Levitical order functioned with the realization of being replaced by the order of Melchizedek. The oath of God guaranteed the promise to Abraham (6:17), and it also secures the priesthood of Christ.

Second, Christ has become the "surety of a better covenant" (7:22). The term "surety" (enguos) is based upon the adverb "near" (engus) and the verb "draw near" (engizō).[7] It connotes the sense of a guarantor, a person who pledges himself. Christ, both by His person and work, is the divine personification of the promise of God to man. He is the one who established the better covenant, the new covenant, through the shedding of His blood. The church ordinance of Communion remembers that significance (Luke 22:20). Christ's return to the earth will finalize the blessings of the new covenant promised to Israel (Jer. 31:31–37; Rom. 11:26–27). His resurrection life and position of advocacy before the Father in heaven can give the believer assurance that he will fully inherit all of the divine promises given to him.

7. The noun is found only here in the New Testament.

III. CHRIST (7:23–28)

The contrast in orders, covering three chapters, now comes to a conclusion. Five superiorities will be presented.

A. He Lives (7:23–24)

The Levitical order consisted of "many priests." There were several jobs which could not be done by one person; thus many priests performed various ministries simultaneously. In addition, there was the constant replacement process. Priests eventually died; thus their positions had to be taken by the new generation (7:23b). There was an intrinsic imperfection within the sacrificial system. One priest by himself could not meet the total needs of one worshiper or of the entire nation. A dead priest naturally could not render any assistance.

On the other hand, the eternal Son of God became man and died, but He rose from the dead. He has an uninterrupted ministry "because he continueth ever" (7:24a). In His infinite compassion, power, and wisdom, He is able to care for all of the needs of all people simultaneously. He can care for each one individually without any limitations. He thus has an "unchangeable" (*aparabaton*)[8] priesthood. The term literally means "not to go beyond." His priesthood can never be replaced or superceded. He can never violate its mission. It has no innate weakness because it depends solely upon a perfect Savior for its fulfillment. Christ needs no help from others. He is the exclusive personification of His eternal order.

B. He Saves (7:25)

The Levitical priest could only offer partial and temporary service within the framework of his own brief lifetime. He had no ability, either innate or imputed, to bring believing sinners into spiritual perfection. He also stood in the need of outside assistance.

8. Used only here in the New Testament.

Four aspects of the redemptive, priestly ministry of Christ are now set forth. First, He alone has the ability to finish what He has begun in the life of a believer. Only He "is able also to save." The verb "able" (*dunatai*)[9] stresses innate power to achieve what He has willed to do. He is able to save because He is the Savior. The performance is a natural extension of His person. The infinitive "to save" (*sōzein*) encompasses salvation in all of its aspects: election, justification, sanctification, and glorification. It extends from eternity past to eternity future. It involves a total restoration to spiritual soundness.

Second, the goal of Christ's salvation is the total perfection of the child of God. The prepositional phrase ("to the uttermost") looks toward the eternal condition of the believer. The term "uttermost" (*panteles*) is based upon two Greek words meaning "all" (*pan*) and "complete" (*teles*). It involves the arrival at the final destination with all aspects of the person completed spiritually. These embrace the body, the mind, the will, and the emotions. In essence, the total personality of the believer will become what God intended in the plan of creation and redemption. The sense of total completeness can be seen in another usage of the term. Jesus healed a crippled woman who "could in no wise [same word] lift up herself" (Luke 13:11). She was totally paralyzed.

Third, the objects of salvation are those "that come unto God by him." The verbal participle "come" (*proserchomenous*) indicates a constant coming of sinners to salvation. Men daily are born again, and Christ will save each one to total perfection. The person who comes does so willingly in obedience to Christ's gracious invitation: "Come unto me, all ye that labour and are heavy laden, and I will give you rest" (Matt. 11:28). He comes because he is the object of divine election, the gift of the Father to the Son (John 6:37). He comes because the Father draws him to the Son (John 6:44–65). God graciously secures the assent of the will of the sinner without violating the responsibility of the accountable person. The means of coming to the Father is exclusively through the person and redemptive work of the Son ("by him"; John 14:6).

9. The English word *dynamite* is based upon this term.

Fourth, the cause of redemptive perfection is the continuous intercession of the resurrected Christ ("seeing he ever liveth to make intercession for them"). On the night before His crucifixion, Christ prayed for believers, His possession which had been given to Him by the Father (John 17:9–10). He interceded for their preservation (John 17:11), sanctification (John 17:17), unity (17:21), and eternal habitation in heaven with Him (John 17:24). In his argument for the ultimate glorification of each chosen believer, Paul appealed to the crucifixion, resurrection, ascension, and prayerful intercession of the Savior (Rom. 8:33–34).

C. He Is Perfect (7:26)

An imperfect Levitical priest could never bring another imperfect person to spiritual perfection. Since Christ is perfect, He can bring imperfect sinners to that goal ("For such an high priest became us"). He is what we need.

Five statements about the superiority of Christ are set forth. First, He is "holy" (*hosios*). Elsewhere He is called the "Holy One" (Acts 2:27; 13:35; same word). The term is ascribed to God (Rev. 15:4). Believers are challenged to manifest such holiness (I Tim. 2:8; Titus 1:8). It stresses an inner purity of thought, emotion, and will.

Second, Christ is "harmless" (*akakos*). The adjective literally means "not bad, wicked, or evil." The word is used only once elsewhere, translated as "simple" (Rom. 16:18). In His relationships with others, Christ is eternally free from malice or craftiness. His motivations are absolutely blameless.

Third, He is "undefiled" (*amiantos*). He has not been morally polluted or stained by outside sinful pressures. The term is used of proper marriage (13:4), religion (James 1:27), and the heavenly inheritance (I Peter 1:4).

Fourth, He is "separate from sinners." Christ ate with publicans and sinners, but He never condoned their sin. He was separated from them, but never isolated from them. He came to seek and to save the lost (Luke 19:10). He wanted to deliver sinners from the practice and penalty of sin. In such contacts with them, His holiness was never diminished. They never influenced Him against that which was morally good.

Fifth, He has come to be "higher than the heavens." He has a priestly ministry in the eternal temple of the presence of God. The earthly temple had been destroyed once, polluted several times, and the priestly system had failed to operate for seventy years during the Babylonian exile (586–516 B.C.). His ministry goes on uninterrupted.

D. He Offered Himself (7:27)

The Levitical priests offered sacrifices "daily." The high priests functioned not just once each year on the Day of Atonement, but they also presented daily offerings. They were to offer "two lambs of the first year day by day continually" (Exod. 29:38). One lamb was sacrificed in the morning; the other in the evening (Exod. 29:39). Each priest knew that he was a sinner, therefore he had to offer "first for his own sins, and then for the people's."

On the other hand, Christ presented *one* sacrifice "once." It never had to be repeated. Its intrinsic value was universal and eternal. Instead of lambs, He offered up "himself." No priest could die for his own sins or for the sins of others, but Christ bore the sins of others (I Peter 2:24).

E. He Has the Oath (7:28)

The Mosaic law established men as high priests even though they had moral, psychological, and physical weaknesses. The term "infirmity" (*astheneian*) denotes these areas rather than a specific illness or disease. They had their own faults. They were not perfect husbands, parents, and citizens, yet they had to serve because the law commanded them to do so.

The divine oath, contained in the Davidic psalm (Ps. 110), was given after the law was codified ("since the law"). It establishes the Son as totally perfected (*teteleiōmenon*) or "consecrated." He has no internal or external flaws.

134

Questions for Discussion

1. Was Melchizedek a real historical person who typified Christ, or was he actually an appearance of Christ in human form? Give arguments, both for and against your position.

2. Are believers under obligation to give a tithe today? Give Scriptural support for your answer.

3. How does the presence of Levi in Abraham contribute to the discussion on abortion? Where does life begin? When?

4. Are believers under all sections of the Mosaic Law today? Or just some parts? Which?

5. What is contained in the hope of the believer? Can it ever be lost?

6. How can believers be holy, harmless, and separate from sinners? What is the difference between isolation and separation?

7. For what does Christ pray in heaven? How do you know? How should that information affect you?

8

The Covenant and the Tabernacle
Hebrews 8:1—9:11

This chapter looks back at the preceding discussion on the priesthood and looks forward to some new contrasts. It begins: "Now of the things which we have spoken this is the sum." Two major comparisons showing the superiority of Christ have already been given: a better position in heaven (4:14-16) and a better order (5:1—7:28). Three more are anticipated: a better covenant (8:1-13), a better sanctuary (9:1-11), and a better sacrifice (9:12—10:18). The term "sum" (*kephalion*) is based upon the Greek word for "head" (*kephalē*). Its only other usage in the New Testament dealt with a sum of money which a Roman captain paid to gain his freedom from slavery (Acts 22:28). In this context, the term refers to the main point or key feature of the present discussion, namely the seated Christ serving out of a heavenly tabernacle and ministering the benefits of the new covenant.

I. THE NEW COVENANT (8:1-13)

The concept of "covenant" (*diathēkē*) will now become a prominent theme in the epistle. It was mentioned only once in the preceding seven chapters, translated as "testament" (7:22). It will be used twelve times in the next two chapters (chaps. 8-9) and four more times in the closing chapters. Of the thirty-three usages in the New Testament, over one half (seventeen) are found in the Book of Hebrews.

A. A Heavenly Ministry (8:1–5)

1. The true tabernacle (8:1–2)

All believers have unlimited access into the presence of God because they constantly have a High Priest who makes that entrance possible. Three descriptions of Christ are given. First, He "is set on the right hand of the throne of the Majesty in the heavens" (8:1b). He assumed this position after He purged our sins (1:3), after He was raised from the dead (Eph. 1:20), and after He ascended from the earth through the heavens (4:14; Acts 1:11; Eph. 4:8–10). Christ Himself asserted that through His redemptive work He overcame and [is] set down with His Father in his throne (Rev. 3:21). As the eternal Son of God, He had an innate right to that exalted position, but as the incarnate God, He gained that privilege through total obedience to the divine will. In His localized human presence within an immortal, incorruptible, resurrected body, He sat down in response to the invitation of the Father (1:13; Ps. 110:1).

Second, He is "a minister of the sanctuary" (8:2a). The English term "liturgy" is based upon the Greek word for "minister" (*leitourgos*). It is later affirmed that Christ has a more excellent "ministry" (*leitourgias*). This concept of service is used elsewhere of the prophets and teachers at Antioch (Acts 13:2), of the material benevolence of Gentile Christians (Rom. 15:27), of the sacrifices of the Jewish priests (9:21; 10:11; Luke 1:23), of government officials (Rom. 13:6), and of angels (1:7). The word "sanctuary" (*tōn hagiōn*) literally reads "the holy things," probably referring to the holy places and furniture of the heavenly temple (Rev. 11:19).

Third, He is a minister of "the true tabernacle." It is true in that it is eternal whereas the earthly tabernacle constructed in the wilderness was a temporary copy (8:5). The true tabernacle is where God dwells, where His glory is manifested (Isa. 6:1–4), where His holiness is acknowledged by angels (Isa. 6:3), and from which His judgment will be executed (Rev. 8:2–6; 11:19; 15:5—16:1). It is also true in that God directly constructed it whereas men made the earthly tabernacle out of animal skins ("which the Lord pitched, and not man"). The metaphor of pitching looks at the fastening of tent pegs. Just as the Mosaic portable tabernacle of skins was replaced by the massive Solomonic temple, so the heavenly tabernacle will be absorbed into the eternal Holy City which will have no temple building. Both "the Lord God Almighty and the Lamb are the temple of it" (Rev. 21:22).

2. The true offering (8:3-4)

Although the sacrifice of Christ is not specifically mentioned in these verses, it is implied through the presentation of three uncontested affirmations. First, "every high priest is ordained to offer gifts and sacrifices." God designated the high priest, and only him, to that human destiny. A priest without a sacrifice would be like a fish without water. Both are suited to each other.

Second, since Christ was ordained of God to be a high priest after the order of Melchizedek, "it is of necessity that this man have somewhat also to offer." The function of Christ's priestly appointment involved not only representation, but also the administration of sacrifice. The fact of offering is vital here, not the object or mode.

Third, Christ could not qualify as a high priest on earth, therefore His priestly functions take place in heaven. The contrary to fact conditional sentence indicates that Christ was in heaven at the time of the writing of the book ("For if he were on earth, he should not be a priest. . .").[1] Since Christ was of the tribe of Judah (7:14), He could not become a Jewish high priest, offer animal sacrifices, nor enter into the holy places of the second temple. During His earthly ministry, He limited His presence to the outer courts of the temple when He visited it in Jerusalem. In the earthly system, the author observed "that there are priests that offer gifts according to the law." The usage of the present verbal tense ("are") shows that the temple was still standing and functioning at the time of the writing of the book, thus it was composed before the destruction of Jerusalem by the

1. The Greek uses *ei* ("if") with a secondary tense *ēn* ("were") in the protasis, and the particle *an* plus the secondary tense *ēn* ("should be") in the apodosis.

Romans (A.D. 70). Under the Mosaic Law, the first covenant (8:7), Christ had no priestly rights or responsibilities. His service thus must be in a heavenly sphere, and the nature of His sacrifice must be radically different from that made by the Jewish priests.

3. The true antitype (8:5)

Many of the Old Testament persons, institutions, and events serve as illustrations of New Testament spiritual truth (I Cor. 10:6, 11). Believers should follow the examples of godly Israelites, but they should avoid the moral failures. In a specialized sense, there are Old Testament concepts which God definitely designed to prefigure the person and redemptive work of Christ. The Old Testament figure is called a type, whereas its New Testament corresponding truth is named an antitype. For example, the qualification and death of the passover lamb which effected the release of Israel from Egyptian bondage provided a picture of the sacrificial death of Christ (I Cor. 5:7).

The earthly service of the Jewish priests thus formed both an "example and shadow of heavenly things." The term "example" (hupodeigmati), used earlier of Israel's example of unbelief (4:11), denotes a copy or a pattern. Christ was an example of humility (John 13:15), Job a pattern of patience (James 5:10), and the fallen angels an example to the ungodly (II Peter 2:6). The concept of "shadow" must be seen in contrast to the substance or body which produces the shadow. A shadow indicates a general form or outline, but there are no distinguishing characteristics evident. Paul charged that the Old Testament regulations of diet, holidays, and sabbaths were a "shadow of things to come; but the body is of Christ" (Col. 2:16–17). The innate essence of the Levitical sacrificial system thus was just a pattern of the heavenly reality which centers in Christ.

At Mount Sinai, God gave Moses specific instructions for the construction of the portable tabernacle: the size, the materials, and the usage (8:5b; Exod. 25:40; 26:30; Num. 8:4). Stephen testified that Moses made it "according to the fashion that he had seen" (Acts 7:44). The term "pattern" (tupon) transliterates as "type." Moses probably saw a visible reproduction of the invisible heavenly temple and recorded the construction details under divine inspiration. Each item or detail thus must have had divine significance even though believers have difficulty in ascertaining it.

B. A Better Ministry (8:6–13)

The connective words ("But now") form the transition from the preceding section to this one. A contrast between the present ministries of Christ and the temple priests will be given. There is also a distinction between what Christ could not have on earth with what He presently enjoys in heaven.

1. He is the mediator of a better covenant (8:6)

Three statements of Christ's superiority are given. First, He has "obtained a more excellent ministry" than the earthly Jewish priests. Their service was partial, interrupted, unproductive, and ceremonial. His is perfect, continuous, effective, and moral. The excellence is based upon His innate perfection, His redemptive sacrifice, and the superiority of the new covenant, which forms the basis of His ministry.

Second, Christ is "the mediator of a better covenant." The old covenant was conditional, based upon man's obedience for its fulfillment, but the new covenant is unconditional, founded upon the faithfulness and integrity of God's pledged word. The old covenant was "ordained by angels in the hand of a mediator," namely Moses (Gal. 3:19). In His person, Christ is better than both the angelic and human mediators of the old system (chaps. 1–3). Paul added, "For there is one God, and one mediator between God and men, the man Christ Jesus" (I Tim. 2:5). Only Christ could qualify for this position because only He was both divine and human.

Third, the new covenant "was established upon better promises." The old system depended upon the promise of man toward God. God challenged Israel at Sinai through Moses:

". . .if ye will obey my voice indeed, and keep my covenant, then ye shall be a peculiar treasure unto me above all people. . ." (Exod. 19:5). The response of Israel was clear: "All that the LORD hath spoken we will do" (Exod. 19:8). Israel had to obey if it wanted to receive the divine blessings. On the other hand, the new covenant stemmed from the unconditional promises of God toward His people. They would receive His blessing because He willed to confer it upon them apart from their merit and solely through His grace.

2. The old covenant had to be replaced (8:7)

The covenants are now contrasted numerically: the first and the second. The author uses the logic of a conditional sentence which expresses a premise which is contrary to fact.[2] The first covenant, the Mosaic Law with its attendant Levitical priestly system, was not "faultless" (amemptos). Since God gave the legal covenant, it was good and perfect in itself (James 1:17). It was truth and achieved its divine purpose. It was never intended to produce justification within the Israelite (Gal. 3:21). The law possessed fault only in that it depended upon man for its fulfillment, and therein was the problem. Paul commented: "For what the law could not do, in that it was weak through the flesh. . ." (Rom. 8:3).

If the first covenant could have imparted eternal life to that person who obeyed it, then why did God promise to give Israel a new covenant? The prediction of the second demonstrates the temporary nature of the first and the replacement of the first by the second.

3. The description of the new covenant (8:8–13)

God found fault with the children of Israel ("with them"), not with the law itself. They disobeyed it continuously for nine hundred years (1500–600 B.C.). Their rebellion characterized the

2. The Greek uses *ei* ("if") with a secondary tense *ēn* ("had been") in the protasis, and the particle *an* plus the secondary tense *ezēteito* ("have been sought") in the apodosis.

time of Moses and Joshua; the period of the judges; the united kingdom under Saul, David, and Solomon; the divided kingdom; and the single kingdom of Judah, which was finally destroyed by the Babylonians (586 B.C.). Jeremiah prophesied during the final days of the Jewish kingdom. Through him, God announced that He would make a new covenant with His people (Jer. 31:31–34). Those promises are repeated in their entirety in this section (8:8–12).

First, the new covenant was not established in the time of Jeremiah; it was only predicted. The time phrase ("the days come") looked forward to the coming of the Messiah–Redeemer.

Second, the new covenant was made with the entire nation of Israel (8:8). After the death of Solomon, the united kingdom of twelve tribes divided into the northern kingdom of ten tribes, called Israel, and the southern kingdom of two tribes, named Judah. Israel was ruled by a series of family dynasties, all wicked and devoted to idolatry. Judah was reigned over by the family of David. Some of the latter kings were godly, whereas others were evil. The temple was located in Jerusalem which was a part of the southern kingdom. The two kingdoms existed beside each other for two hundred years (931–722 B.C.), often in conflict with one another. After Israel was conquered by Assyria (722 B.C.), Judah survived until its defeat by the Babylonians (586 B.C.).

Third, the new covenant is different in essence from the covenant of law given through Moses after the Exodus (8:9). The old covenant was conditional, contingent upon the obedience of the people for the reception of divine blessing. The problem was the repeated historical fact that the Israelites "continued not in my covenant." Their sin brought the chastisement and displeasure of God ("I regarded them not"). The new covenant is based upon God's determinative purpose to change a person's spiritual position and practice.

Fourth, the new covenant will be inscribed within the self, not upon stone (8:10a). The moral absolutes for national Israel were written upon two tables of stone, but God promised: "I will put my laws into their mind, and write them in their hearts."

Fifth, the new covenant produces an eternal, living relationship between God and His people. He stated: "I will be to them a God, and they shall be to me a people" (8:10b). In this entire description, the performance of the covenant rests exclusively upon the divine purpose and power. Note the frequent usage of the intention of the first person ("I will"). The old covenant stressed what man could do for God, whereas the new focuses on what God will do within man.

Sixth, the new covenant emphasizes the divine instruction and illumination of each believer (8:11; Isa. 54:13; John 6:45). There were unsaved who functioned within the framework of the Mosaic covenant, but only the spiritually regenerate will receive the blessings of the new covenant. All will know God through Jesus Christ.

Seventh, the new covenant produces eternal forgiveness of sins (8:12). Under the old system, the "unrighteousness" of men brought the judgment of God to them. The old covenant was a ministration of death and of condemnation (II Cor. 3:7, 9). It demanded total conformity all of the time, and it required a penalty for one violation once (Gal. 3:10; James 2:10). Under the provision of the new covenant, God is "merciful" (*hileōs*) toward the unjust. This term is related to the theological word "propitiation" (*hilasmos;* I John 2:2; 4:10) and the word for the "mercy seat" (*hilastērion;* Rom. 3:25; Heb. 9:5). God could be merciful toward sinners because Jesus Christ satisfied or propitiated the divine demands for the penalty of sin. He "suffered for sins, the just for the unjust" (I Peter 3:18). Christ Himself declared that He would establish the new covenant in His shed blood (Luke 22:20). The result of divine satisfaction with the death of Christ is the total removal of all types of sins. God promised: ". . .their sins and their iniquities will I remember no more."

Eighth, the establishment of the new covenant caused the Mosaic covenant to become old (8:13). The tenure of the first system ended at the crucifixion and resurrection of Christ. The system continued to function within Judaism for forty years (A.D. 30–70), although God was through with it. The imminence of the destruction of the temple by Titus and the Romans (A.D. 70) is indicated by the declaration that the old system was "ready to vanish away." Since that memorable event in the history of the nation, Israel has not reintroduced the sacrificial rites with a functioning Levitical priesthood.

II. THE TABERNACLES (9:1–11)

The previous chapter introduced the subject of the two tabernacles: the heavenly structure (8:2) and the earthly tent (8:5). This passage sets forth the contrast in more vivid detail.

A. The Earthly Tabernacle (9:1–10)

The first covenant was inseparably joined to the Levitical sacrificial system ("ordinances of divine service") which had to function in the appointed place, namely the "worldly sanctuary" (9:1). The adjective "worldly" (*kosmikon*) refers to the geographical location of the building, not to an ethical weakness. Godly priests labored there and spiritual Israelites worshiped there. Its sphere of operation was limited to the present world system of humanity concentrated on planet Earth. The noun "sanctuary" (*hagion*) literally translates as "set apart place" or "holy place." It basically referred to the tent structure within the tabernacle compound marked off by a wall of curtains. The following diagram shows the relative position of the key items:

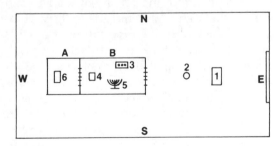

Key

A Most Holy Place
B Holy Place

1 Altar of sacrifice
2 Laver
3 Table of showbread
4 Altar of incense
5 Lampstand
6 Ark of the covenant with mercy seat

1. *Its furniture (9:2-5)*

The tabernacle was divided into two rooms. The "first" room was the area where the priests performed their daily ministries (9:2, 6). It is here called the "sanctuary" (*hagia*). It literally reads "set apart place," or "Holy Place."[3] It was totally dedicated to the worship of the God of Israel. No profane or secular activities were allowed there. In fact, only priests could enter that room; the ordinary believer, whether Jew or Gentile, had no access into that place.

Inside the first room was the "candlestick" which provided the light for that area (Exod. 25:31-39). The candlestick, or lampstand (*luchnia*), was also made according to the divine pattern manifested to Moses. It was made of pure gold, beaten out of one solid piece. It had seven branches with bowls shaped like almonds on each tip to hold oil for burning. The seven branches probably symbolized the calendar week, which pointed back to the creation week.

Across this room was a table on which twelve cakes or loaves of bread were arranged in two rows of six each (Exod. 25:23-30; Lev. 24:5-9). It was made of shittim wood overlaid with gold. The twelve loaves of bread represented the twelve tribes of Israel.

A veil formed the doorway between the two rooms (Exod. 26:31-35). It is here called "the second veil" because the first veil gave entrance into the first room, the Holy Place, from the tabernacle compound where the altar of sacrifice and the laver were located. The second room was called "the Holiest of all" *hagia hagiōn*. It literally reads "Holy of Holies." God manifested His local presence within this second chamber.

The author then stated that the second room had the golden "censer" (*thumiatērion*).[4] On the Day of Atonement, the high priest filled the censer with burning coals of fire from off the sacrificial altar, sprinkled incense upon the coals, and caused the smoke to cover the mercy seat (Lev. 16:12-13). It is possible that

---

3. The relative pronoun "which" (*hētis*) is feminine gender agreeing with its antecedent "tabernacle" (*skēnē*).

4. This word is used only here in the New Testament.

this term may refer to the altar of incense located in the first room in front of the inner veil (Exod. 30:1–10). The close proximity of the altar of incense to the mercy seat and the Holy of Holies would permit the smoke of the incense to penetrate the second chamber. On the Day of Atonement when the high priest pushed aside the veil, the incense smoke would inevitably enter the Most Holy Place.

The "ark of the covenant" was the major piece of furniture within the Holy of Holies. It was a chest made of shittim wood overlaid with pure gold (Exod. 25:10–22). It was about four feet long, two and a half feet wide and high.

Inside the ark were three significant objects from Israel's history. There was a golden pot containing manna, the miraculous food which God provided for Israel during her forty years of wandering in the wilderness (Exod. 16:14–22). The manna was "like coriander seed, white; and the taste of it was like wafers made with honey" (Exod. 16:31). God instructed Moses and Aaron to preserve this pot of manna as a testimony of God's providential care to future generations of Israelites (Exod. 16:32–36).

The chest also contained "Aaron's rod that budded" (9:4b). After the rebellion led by Korah was suppressed, Moses placed twelve rods within the tabernacle. Each rod had a tribal name upon it, and Aaron's name was written upon the rod assigned to Levi. God caused the rod of Aaron to bud, to bloom, and to bear amonds that very day. God then instructed Moses to keep the rod in the ark as a testimony of the divine selection of Aaron to be the high priest (Num. 17:1–13).

The ark also was the container for "the tables of the covenant." The original set of two stone tables that revealed the Ten Commandments inscribed with the finger of God, were broken by the enraged Moses when he witnessed the idolatrous dancing of the Israelites around the golden calf (Exod. 31:18; 32:15–19). God later rewrote the commandments on two new stones, and Moses placed them within the ark (Deut. 10:4–5).

On top of the ark was the "mercy seat" (*hilastērion*). This was sprinkled with the blood of sacrifice on the Day of Atonement (Lev. 16:13–14). It became the place of propitiation, the site where the righteous demands of God for sin were satisfied (Rom. 3:25). Over the mercy seat were the forms of two cherubim, angelic creatures, made of beaten gold (Exod. 25:18–21). They were emblematic of the glory of God, the outward manifestation of the being of God. Over the mercy seat and between the cherubim was the appointed place where God promised to commune with Israel (Exod. 25:22).

The author did not plan to discuss each item of furniture in detail ("of which we cannot now speak particularly"). The relative pronoun "which" (*hōn*) is plural, referring to all of the items that pertained to the earthly tabernacle.

2. Its usage (9:6–7)

After the tabernacle was "ordained" or erected, the priestly duties began. The priests served in the first room, the Holy Place, every day (9:6). They lit the seven lamps on the lampstand every evening and trimmed the wicks each morning (Exod. 27:20–21; 30:7). They burned incense on the altar of incense during the offering of the morning and the evening sacrifices (Exod. 30:7–8). They replaced the twelve loaves of bread on the table of showbread every Sabbath (Lev. 24:5–9).

Only the high priest could go into the second chamber, the Holy of Holies, and he could only enter on one day of the calendar year, the Day of Atonement (9:7). He could not enter "without blood." He actually entered the sacred room twice on that day: the first time to sprinkle the blood of a bullock upon the mercy seat for the atonement of his personal sins and the second time to sprinkle the blood of a goat upon the mercy seat for the atonement of the nation (Lev. 16:11–16). The atonement was made "for the errors of the people." The term "errors" (*agnoēmatōn*) literally reads "no knowledge," referring to the sins of ignorance. A difference was made between sins committed presumptuously and those done out of ignorance, although both were still defined as sins (Num. 15:22–31). No sacrifice could be offered for presumptuous sins.

3. Its limitations (9:8–10)

Whatever God does and says communicates spiritual truth. The divine commands for the construction of the tabernacle and for its service thus were deliberately designed to teach moral concepts and redemptive policy. Three conclusions about the tabernacle liturgy are now given. First, the believer did not have access into the very presence of God (9:8). Since only priests could go into the Holy Place and only the high priest into the Holy of Holies, the people were restricted from entrance into that room where God manifested Himself. It was a vivid reminder that the old covenant, the tabernacle, the priests, and the sacrifices could not bring the Israelites into the presence of God. Through the inspiration of the Old Testament legalistic system, the Holy Spirit was "signifying that the way into the holiest of all was not yet made manifest." Since the tabernacle was a materialistic reproduction of the heavenly pattern, the priests and the people should have known that the Levitical system could not produce spiritual justification or perfection.

Second, the repetition of offering the same sacrifices was a reminder that the real spiritual problem of man could not be solved by physical means (9:9). The tabernacle was a "figure," or literally a "parable" (*parabolē*). Whenever Christ gave a parable, a graphic word story, He admonished His listeners: "He who hath ears to hear, let him hear" (Matt. 13:9). God gave to Israel a functioning parable in the form of the tabernacle worship, but only those whose spiritual eyes had been opened could perceive the true significance of the system. Both the priest and the worshiper should have known that the gifts and sacrifices could not make them "perfect" (*teleiōsai*). Outwardly they knew that they were ceremonially acceptable, but inwardly they recognized that the animal sacrifices did not remove the personal guilt of their sins. Their "conscience" continued to remind them of their trespasses and condemn them.

Third, the old system was simply functioning until its inevitable replacement by the new covenant. Four integral parts of the legalistic code are given special mention: the dietary regulations ("meats"); the controls on beverages ("drinks"); the various ceremonial immersions ("divers washings"); and "carnal ordinances," the judgments which guided social behavior. These all had a cultural, historical, and religious purpose within the framework of the old covenant, but they were temporary. They were to cease at "the time of the reformation." The latter term literally means "to straighten out thoroughly" (*diorthōseōs*). Only the establishment of the new covenant and its inner transformation of the repentant sinner could produce the desired changes. Isaiah declared that the age of the Messiah would do just that: "Prepare ye the way of the LORD, make straight in the desert a highway for our God. Every valley shall be exalted, and every mountain and hill shall be made low: and the crooked shall be made straight, and the rough places plain" (Isa. 40:3-4). This message, proclaimed by John the Baptist, pointed to the advent of Jesus Christ.

B. The Heavenly Tabernacle (9:11)

This verse serves as a fitting transition between the last section, which stressed the covenant and the tabernacle, and the upcoming discussion, which will highlight the sacrifice itself (9:12—10:18). The adversative words ("But Christ") make the abrupt contrast between the Savior and the Jewish priests in the place of ministry and in the nature of the respective sacrifices.

Christ came to be a high priest by divine oath. His appointment anticipated "good things to come," the eternal realities of which the earthly rites are mere symbols.

His tabernacle is "greater" in that it was divinely constructed. It was "not made with [human] hands." It has nothing to do with earthly structures ("not of this building"). It is also "more perfect" (*teleioteras*) in that He can bring the believing sinner to spiritual perfection through the application of His redemptive work. Israelites achieved outward, ceremonial, and social perfection through their system. Christ produces godliness through inward conformity to Himself.

Questions for Discussion

1. What are the blessings of studying the typology of the tabernacle? Dangers? How can a biblical type be detected?

2. How do people today seek to be perfected by the regulations of the old covenant? How do the underlying principles of the old system creep into evangelical circles?

3. How does the new covenant relate to the other covenants: Abrahamic? Palestinian? Davidic?

4. What can men learn about the subject of forgiveness from God? What are its characteristics? Limitations?

5. How does the tabernacle furniture typify Christ? Relate New Testament truths to Old Testament symbols.

6. In what contemporary religions are worshipers shut out of the presence of God? Why are people content to remain in such systems?

7. In what ways is heaven better than earth? In what ways is the heavenly tabernacle better than the earthly?

9

The Perfect Sacrifice
Hebrews 9:12—10:18

In this chapter the contrast between the two priesthoods comes to a climax. The essence of each system involved the sacrifice. Although the death of Christ was mentioned earlier (1:3; 2:9, 14; 7:27), the author did not concentrate on that event in the development of his argument for the superiority of Jesus Christ. He has already shown that Christ has a better position (4:14-16), a better order (5:1—7:28), a better covenant (8:1-13), and a better sanctuary (9:1-11). In a sense, he has saved his best argument for the last. The other superiorities actually are dependent upon the crucifixion, the redemptive sacrifice which He offered.

I. IT REQUIRED CHRIST'S BLOOD (9:12-14)

Animals and humans have blood, but angels and God do not. God is Spirit (John 4:24). The constitution of man is both physical and spiritual. The life principle of the person operates through the organism of the body through the blood. God affirmed that "the life of the flesh is in the blood" (Lev. 17:11). God thus declared that only blood could make an atonement for the soul (Lev. 17:11). God had to become human in order to achieve redemption because He had no blood within His divine nature to shed.

A. The Blood of Animals

1. It was varied

On the Day of Atonement the high priest could not go into the Holy of Holies without blood (9:7). He took the blood of bulls or calves for his own sins and the blood of goats for the sins of the nation (Lev. 16:11, 15).

During the wilderness wanderings, a red heifer "without spot, wherein is no blemish, and upon which never came yoke" was taken outside of the camp and was killed (Num. 19:1–22). The animal was then cremated, and the ashes were mixed with water to form a solution known as the "water of separation" (Num. 19:9). It became a "purification for sin" (Num. 19:9).

2. It purified the flesh

Religious uncleanness within Israel was caused by touching a dead body, by a death within a family, by visiting a family who had just experienced a death, or by touching an uncovered vessel (Num. 19:11–16). To remove that unclean condition, a person had to be sprinkled with the watery ash solution on the third day of the seven-day period of uncleanness. He then would become clean on the seventh day (Num. 19:12). The "purifying of the flesh" produced a ceremonial, social, and cultural acceptance (9:13). It enabled the cleansed person to function once again within Israelite society.

B. The Blood of Christ

1. It gave Christ access into the Holy Place (9:12)

Three features about Christ's entrance into "the holy place" (literally "the holy things" [ta hagia]) can be seen. First, the means of access was "by his own blood," not the blood of dumb animals. Christ's human nature enabled Him to die, and His divine nature gave to that death an infinite value. It was "precious blood," of inestimable value (I Peter 1:19).

Second, He entered "once" into the heavenly Holy Place. The

high priest entered twice on the Day of Atonement, once for his own sins and again for the nation. He also entered every year as long as the tabernacle or temple was standing. His work was never final. Christ's ministry was total and effective, thus He could sit down in the Holy Place (1:3; 10:12).

Third, the basis of Christ's access was the fact that He "obtained eternal redemption." The nature of this redemption (*lutrōsin*) involves release from the penalty of sin and freedom to become all that God wants for His children. Both Zacharias and Anna used this term to depict the work of God through the Messiah to effect the political and spiritual redemption of Israel (Luke 1:68; 2:38). This redemption makes possible divine justification through grace (Rom. 3:24) and the forgiveness of sins (Eph. 1:7). It is "eternal" in both quality and scope.

2. It purged the conscience of men (9:14)

Christ died to "purge" (*katharei*) or to cleanse. Four aspects of that work are set forth. First, the means of cleansing is the blood of Christ. Animal blood could deliver from ceremonial, outward guilt, but His blood cleanses the inner self. The effectiveness is beyond comparison ("how much more").

Second, its basis is the voluntary death of Christ. Animals were passively sacrificed, but Christ actively "offered himself." He was the Good Shepherd who willingly gave His life for His sheep (John 10:11, 15, 17). He was positively holy and negatively sinless. He had no sin principle; He was "without spot" morally (I Peter 1:19). The payment of the redemption price was to God, not to Satan. He functioned as both Priest and sacrifice "through the eternal spirit," a reference to either the Holy Spirit or Christ's own divine, eternal Spirit (John 4:24).[1]

Third, the object of purging was the "conscience from dead works." The legalistic, ritualistic system was dead because it

1. The second view is held by Thomas Hewitt, *The Epistle to the Hebrews* (Grand Rapids: Eerdmans, 1981), p. 148; A. T. Robertson, *Word Pictures in the New Testament* (Nashville: Broadman, 1932), V:400; and Robert W. Ross, "Hebrews," *The Wycliffe Bible Commentary,* Charles F. Pfeiffer and Everett F. Harrison, eds. (Chicago: Moody, 1963), p. 1418.

could not cause a person to pass from spiritual death to life (John 5:24). Only Christ's death could remove the penalty, pollution, and fear of moral guilt and replace it with peace and love (Rom. 5:1; 8:1).

Fourth, the goal of cleansing was service for the living God (9:14b). The believer can function as a priest offering sacrifices of praise, money, and even himself (13:15–16; Rom. 12:1–2; Phil. 4:18; I Peter 2:5, 9).

II. IT REQUIRED CHRIST'S DEATH (9:15–24)

The prepositional phrase ("for this cause") joins this section to the preceding one and advances the discussion on the value of Christ's death. A comparison between the two covenants will again be given. In addition, there will be a contrast in the purification of the two sanctuaries.

A. To Establish the New Covenant (9:15–17)

It was earlier declared that Christ was both the surety and mediator of a better covenant (7:22; 8:6). By human lineage He could not function as a priest under the old covenant. As the "mediator of the new testament" (9:15), Christ established in Himself the fulfillment of the promise in the Abrahamic covenant: ". . .in thee shall all families of the earth be blessed" (Gen. 12:3). The cross, the basis of the new covenant, renders a national blessing to Israel and a universal blessing to all people, both Jews and Gentiles. All who are in the family of God through spiritual regeneration have appropriated the redemptive provisions of the new covenant.

1. The inheritance (9:15)

The first covenant could never remove moral guilt or the penalty of sin, yet people were saved in the ages before the advent of Christ. God was free to justify repentant sinners because the crucifixion of Christ was divinely viewed as a finished work in the eternal decree of redemption. Christ was the Lamb of God slain before the foundation of the world (I Peter 1:20; Rev. 13:8), but historically actualized at the cross. He died "for the redemption of the transgressions that were under the first testament" (cf. Rom. 3:25–26).

All saved men are theologically described as "they which are called" (*hoi keklēmenoi*). God effectually called believing sinners to Himself (I Cor. 1:2, 26–31). He has graciously worked in and through the human will to gain the assent of that will without violating human responsibility. The eternal call of God becomes actualized at the time of personal conversion (Rom. 8:30)

When men are regenerated they "receive the promise of eternal inheritance." They become heirs of God and joint heirs with Christ in the blessings of the Abrahamic and new covenants (Gal. 3:6–9, 29; 4:7). They receive the life of God, guaranteed entrance into the kingdom of God (John 3:3, 5), and an "inheritance incorruptible, and undefiled, and that fadeth not away, reserved in heaven" for them (I Peter 1:4).

2. *The testament (9:16–17)*

The essence of a "testament" (*diathēkē*) or will is that it anticipates the death of the person who makes it (9:16). As long as the testator is alive, the provisions of the will can be changed. It has no power or guarantee during the lifetime of the testator (9:17b).

The will, however, immediately takes on "force" at the death of the testator (9:17a). The term "force" (*bebaia*) emphasizes that which is sure and unchangeable. No codicil can be added to a will after the death of the person who made it.

The death of Christ, who confirmed the will or testament in His blood, thus made the eternal inheritance available to the believing sinner.

B. To Provide Purification (9:18–24)

1. Purification of the old system (9:18–22)

The first testament, the old covenant of law given to Israel through Moses, was "dedicated" (*egkekainistai*) with blood (9:18). It did not become effective until animal blood was shed. The same verb is used of Christ who "consecrated" the new means of access into the presence of God (10:20).

The historical incident of blood inauguration of the legal covenant is now described (9:19–21; Exod. 24:1–8). After Moses had declared the divine precepts, he took the blood, scarlet wool, and hyssop and sprinkled both the book and the people (9:19). The blood was the outward sign of the mutual pledge within the conditional covenant (9:20; Exod. 24:8). In addition, he sprinkled the tabernacle and the liturgical vessels (9:21). The entire sacrificial system of worship was thereby sanctified by the application of animal blood.

The majority of legalistic features was "purged" (*katharizetai*) or cleansed by blood (9:22a). Some poor people received ceremonial purification through the offering of a tenth part of an ephah of fine flour which was not mixed with oil or frankincense (Lev. 5:11–13). Some spoils of war were cleansed by fire and others by water (Num. 31:22–24).

The forgiveness or "remission" (*aphesis*) of sins required the shedding of blood (9:22b). The Greek term for "remission" literally means "to send away from." When God forgives a sinner, He sends away from that person the latter's sins, including the thoughts, acts, penalties, and guilt. The "shedding of blood" implies the death of the sacrificial substitute. The term (*haimatekchusias*) is a double compound word with the literal meaning "the pouring out of blood." When Christ instituted the ordinance of the Lord's Supper in the Upper Room on the evening before His crucifixion, He announced: "For this is my blood of the new testament, which is shed for many for the remission of sins" (Matt. 26:28). The same terms ("blood," "shedding," "remission") are found in both verses.

2. Purification of the new system (9:23–24)

The principle of cleansing has just been declared (9:22); thus it was necessary for the tabernacle to be purified with the blood sacrifices. The Mosaic tabernacle provided the "patterns," the earthly counterpart to the heavenly temple ("things in the heavens").

Since the heavenly sanctuary was superior to the earthly one (9:11), it was necessary that purification would come by "better sacrifices" (9:23b). However, that concept is fulfilled in the one perfect sacrifice of Christ.

Both heaven and the heavenly tabernacle needed to be cleansed because they were "not clean in his sight" (Job 15:15; cf. 25:5). The first sin in the universe was committed by Lucifer in the very throne room of God (Isa. 14:12–17; Ezek. 28:12–19). Heaven thus became tainted by that original sin. Since that time, fallen angels have continued to have access to the presence of God (Job 1:6; Rev. 12:10). The reconciliation of Christ affected both earthly and heavenly things (Col. 1:20). Ultimately, both the present heaven and earth will be burned up to make way for the creation of a new universe (II Peter 3:7–10; Rev. 20:11; 21:1).

After Christ offered Himself, He did not go into "the holy places made with hands," namely the inner sanctuaries of the second temple at Jerusalem. That building with its appurtenances provided the "figures of the true" heavenly temple. Consequently, Christ ascended into heaven, the presence of God, the Holy of Holies within the ideal sanctuary. His purpose was "to appear in the presence of God for us" as our Priest and Advocate (7:25; Rom. 8:34; I John 2:1). There is no indication in Scripture that Christ literally sprinkled His blood in the heavenly presence of God. His blood was poured out on the earth, but He was resurrected so that He could personally represent men before God. In the earthly system, the sacrificial animal did not go into the sanctuary, but its blood was sprinkled on it.

III. IT REQUIRED FINALITY (9:25–28)

The old system dictated multiple deaths of animals, but the new system is predicated upon a single death. This contrast of frequency is set forth in this section.

A. The Old Covenant (9:25–26a)

The high priest of Israel went into the Holy Place many times ("often"). He entered only once each year, but he performed that ministry year after year. His successor maintained that liturgical tradition.

He also went with the "blood of others," namely that of the various animals that were sacrificed yearly. Different animals were killed, but there was no scarcity.

It obviously would have been impossible for Christ to offer Himself often as a sacrifice. A person cannot be killed year after year. The essence of physical death is that it occurs once in a lifetime.

B. The New Covenant (9:26b–28)

1. The First Advent (9:26b)

In contrast to the repetitive ministry of the Jewish priests, God the Son came into the world on one historical occasion to perform one work once. Three concepts of His coming are given. First, the fact of His incarnation is indicated by the verb ("he appeared"). Paul used the same verb when he declared that Christ was God manifest in the flesh (I Tim. 3:16). The verbal form (*pephanerōtai*) stresses the permanent union of the divine and the human natures within His single person.[2] God became human in order to die, but He did not cast off His humanity at His death or resurrection.

Second, the time of Christ's appearance was literally at "the consummation of the ages." The ages which He framed served to prepare the world for His advent (1:2). He definitely came "in the fullness of time" (cf. Gal. 4:4).

2. Perfect middle indicative.

Third, the purpose of Christ's advent was "to put away sin by the sacrifice of himself." Sin was put away in the sense that He disannulled its penalty and power (*athetēsin*). That fact alone shows that the old covenant could not do it. The means for the defeat of sin was the sacrifice of Himself. Christ came "to give his life a ransom for many" (Matt. 20:28).

2. The certainty of death (9:27)

In the normal course of human events, all men will eventually die. Christ raised people from the dead and restored them to natural life, thus they died a second time. These occurrences were unusual, designed within the divine will to manifest the deity of Christ. Present believers have the expectation that they could receive their eternal bodies through immediate translation rather than through death and resurrection (I Cor. 15:51–53; I Thess. 4:17).

Judgment follows death. Believers will be judged at the judgment seat of Christ (II Cor. 5:10) whereas the unsaved will be judged at the great white throne judgment (Rev. 20:11–15).

3. The Second Advent (9:28)

Christ died once, bore the sins of many once, and bore the judgment for those sins once. He completely paid the purchase price for man's redemption from sin. He totally satisfied God's righteous demands for the penalty of sin. He was separated judicially from the Father once (Matt. 27:46). In those hours of darkness, He suffered the judgment of Gehenna. He experienced that eternity of judgment on the cross because His infinite, eternal person was capable of perceiving it.

When Christ returns, He will appear "without sin." When He finished the redemptive sacrifice, God removed from Him the sin of the world. His second advent will not deal with the sin question, because that issue was treated on the cross. Believers are characterized as those "that look for him." This is the look of justifying faith which a repentant sinner exercises when he trusts Christ for deliverance from the penalty and effects of sin.

The "salvation" embraces the total inheritance of the blessings of the new covenant, including an immortal, incorruptible body.

IV. IT REQUIRED OBEDIENCE (10:1–18)

The first mention of the will of God appears in this chapter of the Book of Hebrews (10:7). Thereafter, the noun (*thelēma*) occurs four times (10:9, 10, 36; 13:21) and the verb (*thelō*) four times (10:5, 8; 12:17; 13:18). The perfect sacrifice occurred within the decretive will of God. Peter declared that Christ was "delivered by the determinate counsel and foreknowledge of God" (Acts 2:23). Isaiah prophesied that "it pleased the LORD to bruise" Christ (Isa. 53:10).

A. The Insufficiency of the Sacrificial System (10:1–4)

The law had a "shadow" (*skian*) of the promised salvation ("good things to come"). It provided a dark outline without details. Paul observed that the dietary laws and religious calendar were a "shadow of things to come; but the body is of Christ" (Col. 2:17). The person and redemptive work of Christ were foreshadowed in the types and rites contained within the Levitical system. The old system did create an awareness of sin, the need for a priestly mediator, and the blood offering of an innocent substitute. Christ, consequently, is the "very image" (*eikona*) which produced the shadow. The very nature of the law made it incapable of bringing sinners to spiritual perfection (10:1b).

If any sacrifice or series of offerings could have produced moral maturity, then the priest would have stopped his ministry (10:2a). A person who has been thoroughly and permanently "purged" (*kekatharmenous*)[3] of his sins has a position of perfect acceptance before God. A regenerate person has "no more conscience of sins" in that the moral reproof and conviction of guilt have been removed, even though he still maintains a remembrance of his sinful thoughts and deeds (10:2b).

3. Perfect passive participle.

The repetition of animal sacrifices demonstrated that the priest and the people still had a consciousness of their sins and a guilty conscience concerning them (10:3). Under the provisions of the new covenant, the believer remembers the death of his Savior without any guilty conscience for sins. In the old system, the people remembered their sins with a condemned conscience.

There is both a logical and a theological impossibility in the speculation that animal blood could take away sins (10:4).[4] The verb ("take away") literally means "to lift up away from" (*aphairein*). God promised Israel that He would take away their sins through the institution of the new covenant (Rom. 11:27). Common sense also dictates that the blood of a goat could not remove the sin of murder, cleanse the conscience from guilt, and impart eternal life.

B. The Sufficiency of Christ (10:5–18)

1. He did the will of God (10:5–9a)

First, Christ did the will of God by becoming incarnate (10:5). He came into the world of mankind from outside of it (John 1:9). He was God the Son, co-equal with the Father and the Spirit in the Trinitarian divine being. In His divine consciousness He knew that no sacrifice or offering could satisfy the God of justice. He therefore condescended to take upon Himself a true and perfect human nature, including a body of flesh, bone, and blood. The author confirmed this resolution of the Son by his quotation from a Davidic psalm (Ps. 40:6–9). By the Spirit of God, he gives an extension and an interpretation of the Hebrew text which reads: "Mine ears hast thou opened [bored or digged]. . ." (Ps. 40:6).[5] The piercing of the ears depicted the ceremony in which a slave pledged his service to his master rather than accept freedom (Exod. 21:5–6). The acceptance of incarnation, therefore, was the pledge of the Son to the Father to become the obedient Suffering Servant.

4. The term "impossible" (*adunaton*) is emphasized in this verse, occurring at the very beginning of the sentence.
5. The Septuagint, however, has the reading found in the King James Version.

Second, Christ manifested His obedience by His willingness to die on the cross (10:6–9a). The eternal Son of God knew two basic concepts about the holiness of God and the sinfulness of man. He knew that God took no "pleasure" (*eudokēsas;* 10:6, 8) in animal sacrifices in that they could never satisfy His justice, His righteous demands for deliverance from the penalty of sin. Although God commanded the offering of blood sacrifices within the Mosaic covenant, He never accepted them as the basis of divine justification. Christ also knew that God did not will decretively ("thou wouldest not"; *ēthelēsas;* 10:5, 8) that various sacrifices would be the payment price for sin. Four types are mentioned here: "sacrifice" (*thusian*), either the peace or trespass sacrifice; "offering" (*prosphoran*), probably the meal offering; "burnt-offerings" (*holokautōmata*); and "sin" offering (*peri hamartias*).

In total awareness of the eternal plan of redemption and the revealed statements of messianic Scripture, Christ willed to come to do the will of God (10:7, 9). When David wrote his psalm (Ps. 40), the "volume of the book" referred to the five books of the Law. The term "volume" (*kephalidi*) literally means "head" and refers to the knob at the end of the roller around which the manusript of the Scriptures was wound. From the standpoint of the Incarnation, it undoubtedly includes the entire Old Testament (Luke 24:27, 44). After His resurrection, Christ expounded all of those passages which revealed the nature and necessity of His crucifixion.

2. He established the new covenant (10:9b)

Through the cross Christ accomplished two objectives. First, He took away the first covenant with its legalistic code and sacrificial system. The believer is under no obligation to the Mosaic Law made for Israel (Rom. 6:14; Gal. 5:1). Christ did not come to improve the law, but to fulfill it. That system, as a shadow and type, pointed to Him. That righteousness which the law demanded is imputed to the believer in Christ through the provision of the new covenant (Rom. 10:4–11). Christ Himself said that He did not come to patch up the rips of the old system or to put the new wine of His teaching into the old wineskins of Judaistic traditionalism (Matt. 9:16–17).

Second, Christ established the second covenant, the new system in His own redemptive sacrifice.

3. He sanctified believers (10:10)

The will of God for Christ involved the positional sanctification of all believers ("by the which will"). This theological concept is stressed throughout this book as a part of the divine redemptive plan (2:11; 10:10, 14, 29; 13:12). The verb "sanctify" (*hagiazō*) applies to four different stages of the believer's salvation. It refers to the ministry of the Holy Spirit in the person's life before conversion (Gal. 1:15; II Thess. 2:13); the time of regeneration (I Cor. 1:2; 6:11); the present cleansing of the Christian by the Spirit through the Scriptures (John 17:17); and the total separation from the effects of sin when the believer receives the incorruptible, immortal body (Eph. 5:26–27).

The emphasis of this verse is upon the permanent position of sanctification ("we are sanctified"; *hēgiasmenoi esmen*).[6] It looks back to the time of conversion when a person became set apart unto God and views the present resultant standing of that transforming decision. The means of this sanctification was the non-repeatable offering of Christ.

4. He finished His sacrificial work (10:11–13)

This passage contains a series of obvious contrasts between the unfinished work of the Jewish high priests and the finished redemptive work of Christ. First, the legal system had many priests ("every priest"), but the new covenant needs only one ("this man").

Second, the priests always stood in their service ("standeth"), but Christ "sat down on the right hand of God" after He offered Himself. There were no chairs in the Mosaic tabernacle or

6. It is a periphrastic construction with the usage of the present tense of *eimi* ("to be") with the perfect passive participle.

Solomonic temple. The posture indicated an interminable ministry. The seating of the Savior, on the other hand, indicates the completion of His task (1:3, 13).

Third, the work of the priests went on "daily," even on the sabbaths, but Christ completed His work in one day, namely the hours of His crucifixion.

Fourth, the priests were continually "ministering and offering," but Christ "offered" only one sacrifice once.[7]

Fifth, the priests offered "oftentimes the same sacrifices," but Christ offered just "one" sacrifice.

Sixth, the value of each sacrifice under the old system lasted only until the repetition of that sacrifice. It thus was temporary, but the value of Christ's death will last "forever."

Seventh, the animal sacrifices could "never take away sins," but Christ produced a perfect vicarious atonement when He suffered "for sins." The verb ("take away") literally means "to lift up from around" (*perielein*).[8] It connotes expiation. The verbal concept is based upon the metaphor of stripping off a soiled garment closely wrapped around a body.

Eighth, the priests perceived no ultimate triumph from their ministry, but Christ fully expected that His death and resurrection would eventually establish the kingdom of God on earth (10:13). Christ viewed His own crucifixion as a victory to achieve over Satan and sin (I Cor. 15:24–28).

5. *He perfected believers (10:14)*

Through the cross Christ "perfected" every believer. The verb (*teteleiōken*) focuses on the event of regeneration and the permanent standing of spiritual completeness which resulted from conversion.[9] Each believer has positional perfection in Christ, although he must advance toward maturity in his daily practice. Before God the believer is as perfect today as he will be in eternity future. God supplied in the death of Christ all that men need to have a perfect position before Him.

---

7. Note the difference in the tenses: present ("offering"; *prospheron*) and aorist ("offered"; *prosenegkas*).

8. Aorist infinitive of *periaireō*.

9. Perfect active indicative.

The title for believers is literally "them that are being sanctified" (*tous hagiazomenous*).[10] It can denote either men who are progressively advancing in their Christian experience (practical sanctification) or the constant evangelism of men who are getting saved every day (positional sanctification).

6. He forgave sins (10:15–18)

The author concludes his argument with another quotation of the new covenant. He ascribes it to the Holy Spirit (10:15) even though Jeremiah attributed it to Jehovah (Jer. 31:31). The Holy Spirit, of course, is divine and thus can claim the name of Jehovah which can properly be designated to all three persons of the divine being. In another sense, even if God the Father originally announced the new covenant to Jeremiah, the Holy Spirit superintended the prophet in the actual writing of the promises (II Peter 1:20–21).

The old covenant objectively contained the laws of moral absolutes on inanimate stone tablets, but through the provisions of the new covenant, God can subjectively implant His holy standards on the inner self of each repentant believer (10:16).

Another benefit of being under the new covenant is the total removal and judicial forgiveness of all sins (10:17). In what sense does God no longer "remember" sins? In His omniscience, He is aware of them, but He will not hold those sins against the person. Christ died for those sins: their cause, their occurrence, and their effects. The people are no longer judicially culpable. God will not exact any penalty from them because Christ bore that punishment as their substitute.

The possession of "remission" automatically negates the further need of any more "offering for sin" (10:18). The logic is simple and direct. If God has totally removed and forgiven the sins of a believer, the Christian does not have to offer animal sacrifices because he is judicially sinless and accepted in Christ. The temple system with its priests, sacrifices, and liturgical calendar could contribute nothing to the further positional

10. Present passive participle.

perfection and sanctification of the child of God. In fact, the willingness to remain within the Levitical system would be an alarming distraction and obstacle to genuine development of spiritual maturity (6:1).

Questions for Discussion

1. What contemporary religions still use blood sacrifices in their worship? What parallelisms are there between them and Israel? How can they be reached with the gospel?

2. If a person still claims to have a guilty conscience after he has professed faith in Christ, what can be done to help him? What is the difference between guilt feelings and genuine moral guilt?

3. What is the difference between modern wills and the testament of Christ? Can both be contested? Can an inheritance be refused?

4. How does the Roman Catholic concept of the mass violate the biblical view of Christ's death? Discuss other views on the ordinance of the Lord's Supper.

5. What sacrifices should believers offer today? What are the functions of a believer–priest?

6. How do positional perfection and sanctification support the doctrine of the eternal security of the believer? How do those who deny security approach these concepts?

7. What is the difference between divine and human remembrance of sins? What can be learned about forgiveness from God?

10

The Time for Decision
Hebrews 10:19–39

At this point in the Book of Hebrews the argument for the superiority of Jesus Christ is basically over (1:1—10:18). Throughout this major section exhortations and warnings were frequently inserted to stimulate the readers to advance toward spiritual maturity. The author now will concentrate on the practical application of the truth that has just been revealed. It is the time for decision, for positive resolution, and for taking a stand in divine grace.

I. EXHORTATIONS (10:19–25)

The conjunction ("therefore") joins this passage to the preceding material. The vocative ("brethren") is also designed to catch the attentiveness of the readers. This is the first time since the third chapter of Hebrews (3:1, 12) that the author has directly addressed them as his brothers in the family of God. This paragraph is built around three major exhortations (10:22, 23, 24). They all stress constant, accountable activity, and in all of them the author includes himself with his readers as subjects of obedience ("Let us. . .").[1]

---

1. All three are hortatory subjunctives, present active. The first is in the middle voice, but is deponent, thus having active meaning.

A. Their Basis (10:19–21)

The participle ("having") stresses continuous possession and relationship and also indicates the cause or stimulus for spiritual steadfastness and advancement. It could be translated: "Because we have..., let us...."[2] The proof for the possession was demonstrated in the argument section (1:1—10:18). Two blessings enjoyed by the believer are isolated: right of access into God's presence (10:19–20) and the priestly ministry of Christ (10:21).

1. Boldness (10:19–20)

The term "boldness" (parrēsian) is found four times in this book, translated elsewhere as "confidence" or "boldly" (3:6; 4:16; 10:19, 35). It is a compound word literally meaning "speech beside." It connotes the freedom to express orally the concerns and requests of the heart, not an arrogant, aggressive outspokenness. It also depicts the opportunity to address a superior apart from personal fear and apprehension. The believer thus has such boldness "to enter into the holiest," namely the heavenly presence of God. The average Israelite could not go into the earthly Holy of Holies; thus he depended upon the priests as his intercessors. The means of access is "the blood of Jesus." The high priest did not go into the tabernacle apart from blood, and so the child of God goes before God through the merit of Christ's redemptive work.

The terms "way" (hodon) and "enter" (eisodon) are both built upon the same word stem. The path of access is described in five ways. First, it is "new" (prosphaton).[3] In its derivation, the adjective meant "freshly killed." The priests of Israel offered the same sacrifices year by year, but Christ's death was unique, fresh, a type of sacrifice that never existed before.

Second, the way of access is "living" (zōsan). If the first adjec-

2. It is seen as a causal participle, present tense.
3. Used only here in the New Testament.

tive focused on Christ's crucifixion, then this descriptive word points to His resurrection. Christ Himself declared, "I am the way, the truth, and the life: no man cometh unto the Father, but by me" (John 14:6). He was the living one who died but who became alive "for evermore" (Rev. 1:18). He was the slain lamb who stood in triumph (Rev. 5:6).

Third, Christ "consecrated" (*enekainisen*) or dedicated the way for believers by shedding His blood (9:18). Only the giving of His life in death could sanctify forever the new covenant and the means of access into God's holy presence.

Fourth, the way is seen as "the veil." The veil separated the two sections of the Mosaic tabernacle (9:3). It was pulled aside by the high priest only on the Day of Atonement. The veil in the second temple, which was destroyed by the Romans, consisted of a huge tapestry: sixty feet long, thirty feet high, and six inches thick. When Christ died, God ripped this temple veil in two, from the top to the bottom (Matt. 27:51).

Fifth, the tabernacle veil was a type of Jesus Christ. His "flesh" (*sarkos*), or His very humanity, constituted the antitype, the prophetic fulfillment of that which the inanimate veil symbolized. God the Son became incarnate. He "was made flesh" and tabernacled among men in order to bring men to the Father through Himself (John 1:14).

2. High priesthood of Christ (10:21)

All believers, both Jews and Gentiles, have Christ as their high priest. He represents them before God and in Him they have an acceptable, judicial standing. The priests of Israel were in charge of Israel with its tabernacle, but Christ is over the total house of God (3:6). God today dwells in heaven but He also resides within each believer. Collectively, all Christians constitute "a spiritual house, an holy priesthood, to offer up spiritual sacrifices, acceptable to God by Jesus Christ" (I Peter 2:5). As the priest after the order of Melchizedek, Christ reigns over the church, the "royal priesthood" (I Peter 2:9).

B. Their Description (10:22-25)

It is one thing to have spiritual possessions (10:19-21); it is another to enjoy them (10:22-25). The former is based upon Christ's objective work, whereas the latter is tied to the subjective response of obedience within the believer. Three basic commands are enjoined upon the believers.

1. Let us draw near (10:22)

The first exhortation relates to the believer in his approach to God. Four features can be seen. First, he must draw near "with a true heart." He must come with genuine sincerity, void of hypocrisy and ritualistic conformity. Solomon cautioned, "Keep thy heart with all diligence; for out of it are the issues of life" (Prov. 4:23).

Second, he must come "in full assurance of faith." Earlier the author wanted them to manifest the full assurance of hope (6:11). The words "full assurance" (*plerophoriāi*) characterized Abraham's faith in the power and promise of God to give him a son (Rom. 4:21). They described the doctrinal truth which was "most surely believed" [same word] by Luke and his companions (Luke 1:1). They should mark the believer in his exercise of Christian liberty (Rom. 4:21; "fully persuaded"; same word). This inner conviction must have its source in total faith and should be saturated by continuous trust in the revealed will of God.

Third, believers must approach God with "hearts sprinkled from an evil conscience." Only the redemptive work of Christ applied through regeneration can produce a good conscience (I Tim. 1:5). When the blood of the Savior is sprinkled upon the inner self, metaphorically speaking, He purges it and makes it judicially clean (9:14; I Peter 1:2).

Fourth, Christians should draw near with their "bodies washed with pure water." The body is not literally washed with water any more than the heart is sprinkled with actual blood. This symbolical language is based upon the Levitical purification rites (Exod. 29:21; 30:19-21; Lev. 8:6-23). In Ezekiel 36:25 we read,

"Then will I sprinkle clean water upon you, and ye shall be clean: from all your filthiness, and from all your idols, will I cleanse you." The participle "washed" (*leloumenoi*) speaks of the washing of regeneration (Titus 3:5). The "pure water" is the Word of God in contrast to the literal water used by the priests (John 15:3; Eph. 5:26).

2. Let us hold fast (10:23)

The verb literally means "to have down" (*katechōmen*). The metaphor connotes a thorough possession. It was used twice earlier (3:6, 14). In the parable of the Sower Christ declared, "But that on the good ground are they, which in an honest and good heart, having heard the word, keep [*katechousi;* same word] it, and bring forth fruit with patience" (Luke 8:15). The possession is the evidence of genuine salvation (I Cor. 15:2).[4]

Three aspects of the exhortation can be observed. First, the object of holding fast is literally "the confession of the hope" (*tēn homologian tēs elpidos*). This is the confession of faith in the deity of Christ, in His sacrificial work on the cross, and in His resurrection. All believers are "saved by hope" in that they have committed their trust to God, who controls their future (Rom. 8:24).

Second, the attitude of holding must be "without wavering" (*aklinē*).[5] The term literally means "no leaning." It stresses that which is firm and unbending. The metaphor is of a structure with an anchored foundation which will not be moved by tremendous wind currents. The author did not want the pressures of an aggressive Judaism to sway his readers.

Third, the basis of the exhortation is the faithfulness of God. Paul wrote: "Faithful is he that calleth you, who also will do it" (I Thess. 5:24). Abraham knew that God was able to perform what He had promised (Rom. 4:21). God does not lie, therefore the child of God can rest in His pledged word, the redemptive blessings of the new covenant.

4. The same verb is translated here: "keep in memory."
5. Used only here in the New Testament.

3. Let us consider (10:24–25)

The third exhortation relates the readers to their fellow believers. The command to "consider" (*katanoōmen*) implies thoughtful perception and serious concern. It was earlier used of a proper contemplation of Christ (3:1).

The immediate goal of this mental resolution was the provocation of others. The English infinitive phrase ("to provoke") is actually the translation of a Greek prepositional phrase "into provocation" (*eis paroxusmon*). It transliterates as "paroxysm." It is based upon two words which mean "to sharpen beside," thus it implies stimulation or incitement. Such provocation can be either good or bad. On the negative side, the "contention" (same word) between Paul and Barnabas was so severe that they separated from each other in their missionary ministries (Acts 15:39). Genuine love "is not easily provoked" (I Cor. 13:5). Positively, Paul's spirit was "stirred" (same word) when he viewed the idolatry of Athens (Acts 17:16). Solomon gave this counsel: "Iron sharpeneth iron; so a man sharpeneth the countenance of his friend" (Prov. 27:17). The latter meaning, of course, was the author's intention.

The two areas of provocation are "unto love and to good works." The former deals with the inner attitude of the heart whereas the latter focuses on observable performance.

The means of provocation are two: association and exhortation (10:25). The pressure of ostracism and the threat of bodily harm had caused some not to attend the congregational meetings of the local church ("as the manner of some is"). The early believers in Jerusalem were together, continuing in fellowship and apostolic instruction (Acts 2:42–44). Weakness comes through division, but togetherness fosters unity and strength. There can be no mutual encouragement if there is separation. Personal interaction of ministry is absolutely necessary. Each member of the body needs the other members (I Cor. 12:12–26).

The urgency of assembly and comfort was prompted by the historical situation: ". . .and so much the more, as ye see the day approaching." There is much dispute over the meaning of the day. Most commentators view it as the day of Christ's return.

That day is imminent, but can any believer see it approaching? On the other hand, Jesus predicted that Jerusalem would fall to the Gentiles and that the temple would be destroyed (Matt. 24:1-2). The hostilities which led to the Jewish-Roman War (A.D. 66-73) were now upon the readers. The pressure from Judaism upon converted Jews would mount as the defense of Jerusalem became inevitable. That prophetic fulfillment could be detected by the discerning saint. He had to be faithful to Christ even though he knew his beloved city would be destroyed by the pagan Romans.

II. WARNING (10:26-31)

This warning must be seen within the context of exhortations given to genuine believers (10:19-25; 10:32-39). The author included himself within the warning ("we"; 10:26), although later he restricted the possible failure to an isolated individual ("he," 10:29). This written caution thus is not addressed to unbelievers. It must be approached from the same exegetical perspective found in all of the exhortations and warnings scattered throughout the epistle.

A. The Nature of Judgment (10:26-29)

The conjunction ("for") joins the warning of possible judgment to the previous three commands.

1. The sin (10:26)

The emphasis is on constant repetition of sin.[6] It is not sin done out of ignorance, but "wilfully" (*ekousiōs*), deliberately, with full understanding of the nature of the sin and its consequences. It is proverbially "first degree" sin. The term is used elsewhere of Philemon's willingness to receive Onesimus (Philem. 14) and

6. The verb is actually a present participle, translated in the KJV with conditional meaning (cf. 6:6).

173

of an appointment to the position of elder undertaken willingly (I Peter 5:2). In this context, it is gross disobedience to the expressed exhortations: a failure to draw near, to hold fast, and to consider (10:22–24). The seriousness of the sin is increased by the reception "of the knowledge of the truth," namely the superiority of Christ in His person and sacrificial work (1:1—10:18). Sinning without the impartation of all of the facts is bad, but sinning when all of the divine truth has been revealed is worse.

The enigmatic conclusion simply means that there was no Levitical sacrifice which could remove presumptuous sin. In addition, there was nothing more that Christ could do to remedy their situation. A move into maturity would bring them the benefits of the abundant life, but a deliberate refusal to do so would only produce chastisement. Asaph, the psalmist, wondered about the judgment of God upon Israel thusly: "How long LORD? wilt thou be angry for ever? shall thy jealousy burn like fire?" (Ps. 79:5).

The rebel who "despised Moses' law died without mercy under two or three witnesses" (10:28; Deut. 17: 5–6). To despise is to set at nought, to reject, to render as inoperative in one's own life (*athetēsas*). The rebel died by stoning. There was no opportunity to repent, to make restitution, or to offer a sacrifice. There was no mercy extended to him. The analogy should be apparent. Christ is better than Moses and the new covenant is superior to the law, thus the rebel within the Christian assembly can likewise expect severe chastisement, even physical death.

A rhetorical question is now directed to the readers ("suppose ye"; 10:29). The author fully expected that his readers would come to the same answer as the one recorded. A violator of the new covenant would be subject to "much sorer punishment." The adjective "sorer" (*cheironos*) is elsewhere always translated as "worse" (Matt. 9:16; 12:45; 27:64; Mark 2:21; 5:26; Luke 11:26; John 5:14; I Tim. 5:8; II Tim. 3:13; II Peter 2:20). The noun "punishment" (*timōrias*) is found only here in the New Testament, but its verbal form is used twice of physical penalty only (Acts 22:5; 26:11).

What is the exact nature of this punishment? Views differ.

Some see it as the judgment of the lake of fire for apostates. Others view it as severe chastisement at the hand of God in this life attended by the loss of reward at the judgment seat of Christ (Acts 5:1–11; I Cor. 3:13–15; 11:27–34).[7] In the second instance it could even involve divine permission for Satan to afflict the child of God (Luke 22:31–34; I Cor. 5:5; I Tim. 1:20). A violator of the old covenant suffered at the hands of men, but a rebel under the new covenant will be dealt with directly by God (10:30–31). This comparison shows why the punishment for the second type of violation is worse.

The sin of this violator has three features. First, he "has trodden under foot the Son of God." This verbal imagery was used in the parable of the Sower when seed was stepped upon on the wayside (Luke 8:5), of the savorless salt which was cast out upon the ground (Matt. 5:13), of the pigs who trample pearls under their feet (Matt. 7:6), and of people who selfishly and carelessly pushed and shoved each other in their haste to follow Christ (Luke 12:1). In this context, the neglect and disregard of the Savior constitutes a metaphorical trampling.

Second, he has "counted the blood of the covenant, where-with he was sanctified, an unholy thing." The possession of salvation is definitely indicated by the fact that the person "was sanctified (*hēgiasthē*)[8] At conversion he was forever set apart from the world unto God (I Cor. 1:2; 6:11). Sanctified people are saved people. The adjective "unholy" (*koinon*) is better translated as "common."[9] When a believer lives his life with indifference toward the cross, he simply treats it as a mere historical event with no impact upon his decisions.

Third, he "has done despite unto the Spirit of grace." Else-where the verb (*hubrizō*) stresses shameful treatment of persons (Matt. 22:6; Luke 11:45; 18:32; I Thess. 2:2). Here the verb has the prefix "in" (*enubrisas*). The Holy Spirit dwells within each sanctified believer, and the child of God can grieve and quench Him when he refuses to submit to His guidance and authority (Eph. 4:30; I Thess. 5:19).

7. Author's opinion.
8. Aorist passive indicative.
9. The language of the New Testament is *Koine* Greek, the Greek of the common man in the first century.

B. Source of Judgment (10:30–31)

In this age, believers are not the instruments to mete out physical punishment upon the rebels within a local church (Rom. 12:17–21). Within Israel the leaders had the civil responsibility of corporeal punishment.

Two citations from the Old Testament are given to prove that only God can properly judge His own. The first shows that vengeance is the sole prerogative of God (Deut. 32:35; Rom. 12:19). The second asserts that "the LORD shall judge his people" (Deut. 32:36; Ps. 135:14). The reference to the Lord's people further substantiates the position that the judgment under discussion is not the eternal punishment of the lost, but rather the chastisement of erring children within the covenant. The two passages from Deuteronomy were given by Moses to Israel just before the nation advanced into the Promised Land. They served as a warning to obey God out of sincere reverence for His holy being.

The conclusion of the warning is obvious (10:31). The living God is aware of presumptuous sin within His people and will judge accordingly. All believers thus should work out the expression of their salvation "with fear and trembling" (Phil. 2:12). After Ananias and Sapphira died prematurely for their deliberate sins, "great fear came upon all the church" (Acts 5:11). Christ instructed His disciples not to fear man, but God (Matt. 10:26–31).

III. EVALUATION (10:32–39)

This section is marked off by two grammatical features: two conjunctions ("but," 10:32; and "therefore," 10:35) and two commands ("call to remembrance," 10:32; and "Cast not away," 10:35). From the perspective of their present experience, the readers are exhorted to look back to their past spiritual achievements (10:32–34) and then to look ahead with enduring faith (10:35–39).

A. Past Victories (10:32–34)

The imperative stresses constant mental rehearsal. It could be translated: "Keep on reminding yourselves" (*ana-mimnēskesthe*).[10] The object of their attentive review was their "former days," the time period immediately following their conversion to Christ.

1. Their conversion (10:32a)

The conversion of the readers is identified as the time when they "were illuminated" (*phōtisthentes*).[11] This verbal description was used in an early warning (6:4). It stresses that work of God when He opens up the eyes of spiritual understanding for those who were blinded in their sin by Satan (II Cor. 4:4, 6; Eph. 1:18). It points to an instantaneous event when the believing sinner passes from darkness to light.

2. Their courage (10:32b–33)

Right after the readers were saved, they "endured a great fight of afflictions." The English "athlete" is the transliteration of the Greek word for "fight" (*athlēsin*).[12] The verbal form (*athleō*) is translated as "strive" elsewhere (II Tim. 2:5). They immediately became engaged in a spiritual contest with Satan, the demons, and the world of unregenerate men. The fight resulted in "afflictions," or "sufferings," (*pathēmatōn*) for them. Just as Christ became perfect through suffering, these believers could mature in the will of God if they maintained their obedience (2:9–10). In so doing, they could enter into the fellowship of the Savior's sufferings (Phil. 3:10).

The readers' afflictions were both direct and indirect (10:33). They personally "were made a gazingstock" (*theatrizomenoi*).[13] The English term "theater" is based upon this term (*theatron;* Acts 19:29, 31). In his evaluation of the ridicule he received, Paul

10. Present middle imperative.
11. Indicated by the aorist tense of the participle.
12. Found only here in the New Testament.
13. Found only here in the New Testament.

declared that he was made a "spectacle" (*theatron*) to the world of angels and men (I Cor. 4:9). The analogy is clear. The Christians were viewed as foolish clowns on the stage of life. Just as observers would hurl both verbal abuse and material objects at rejected actors, so the unsaved cast two types of persecution upon the believers. The first consisted of "reproaches" (*oneidismois*), namely oral ridicule and mockery. On the cross Christ suffered such barrages of vocal insults (Matt. 27:39–44). Later the author challenged his readers to bear nobly the reproach of Christ in their identification with Him (11:26; 13:13; Rom. 15:3). The second form was "afflictions" (*thlipsesi*), actual hurt to both person and property. Christ promised that His own would experience this type of tribulation (John 16:33; same word).

They became indirectly involved in the persecutions of others when they willingly associated themselves with other suffering saints (10:33b). They became "companions" (*koinōnoi*), sharing in the fellowship of suffering for Christ.

3. Their compassion (10:34a)

The author at one time had been in prison ("in my bonds").[14] The readers "had compassion" (*sunepathēsate*) on him. This verb transliterates as "sympathize." It was earlier used of Christ, who suffers along with us in our infirmities (4:15). All believers should develop such reciprocal compassion (I Peter 4:8). When Paul was about to face martyrdom in his second imprisonment at Rome, he commended Onesiphorus for his visits and courageous association (II Tim. 1:16–18).

4. Their conviction (10:34b)

The unsaved spoiled or seized the material goods of the believers. The response of the believers was not natural; rather it manifested their control by the Holy Spirit when they took the action "joyfully" (Gal. 5:22). The cause of this inner joy was the absolute conviction of heart and mind that no one could take away their eternal inheritance. It was "better and enduring,"

14. Some Greek manuscripts read "their bonds."

whereas earthly possessions are merely inferior and temporary. As Christ had instructed, they had stored heavenly treasure (Matt. 6:19-21). Temporary inconvenience must be seen as just that; their eyes were fixed on God and heaven.

B. Future Needs (10:35-39)

The past victories had become a blurred memory in the readers' present ambivalence. They needed to redefine their goals. The author thus sought to encourage them in their necessary advance toward maturity.

1. Confidence (10:35)

The negative imperative stresses the prevention of such action. It could be translated, "Do not begin to cast away" (*mē apobalēte*).[15] It is used elsewhere of the blind beggar who flung away his worthless coat when Jesus called him (Mark 10:50).

The "confidence" (*parrēsian*) is both objective and subjective. It points to the established access of the believer into the presence of God through Christ (4:16; 10:19) and to the inner conviction of heart that one is in the truth (3:6).

The "great recompense of reward" is not eternal life or heaven. Rather, the utilization of confidence produces the abundant life which embraces the glorification of God, personal joy, and answered prayer (John 15:7-11). When a believer abides in Christ through total submission, then he takes advantage of the confidence afforded to him. John added, "And this is the confidence [same word] that we have in him, that, if we ask any thing according to his will, he heareth us" (I John 5:14). Divine response to the human need thus is the great reward.

2. Patience (10:36-37)

The author claimed that they had "need of patience," the ability to remain or abide under the pressures imposed on them.

15. Indicated by the negative *mē* with the aorist subjunctive.

The patience was necessary in the very doing of the will of God. To do the will of God, in the context of this book, is to obey the many exhortations. The reception of the promise comes after obedience, not before or during it. The "promise" does not refer to eternal life, but rather to the full blessings of the abundant life (10:23). Paul encouraged his readers: "And let us not be weary in well doing: for in due season we shall reap, if we faint not" (Gal. 6:9).

At this point the author inserted a verse from the Book of Habakkuk (10:37; Hab. 2:3). The Old Testament prophet wondered why God delayed in sending His judgment upon Israel for her sins. God assured him that it would come and that he should patiently wait for it. In like manner, the readers were to view both the coming of Christ and the destruction of the temple system as imminent events.

3. Faith (10:38)

A "just" (*dikaios*) person is one who has been declared to be righteous because he has been made righteous in Christ (Rom. 5:1). The justified believer then lives by faith. A person exercises saving faith when he initially places his trust in Christ and continues to leave it there.

When a professing believer draws back, he withdraws his alleged trust in Christ. That action demonstrates that he never exercised justifying faith. His defection demonstrates his absence of salvation, not a loss of eternal life (I John 2:19). God has no pleasure in these apostates.

4. Perseverance (10:39)

Judas Iscariot was the perfect example of a professing believer who drew back into perdition. Christ called him "the son of perdition" (John 17:12). Although Judas identified himself socially and religiously with Christ and the apostolic group, he never was saved (John 13:10-11). He never was a gift from the Father to the Son in the eternal decree of election (John 6:37; 17:9-10). The withdrawal was the evidence of an unregenerate heart, and the destination of all lost men is "perdition" (*apōleian*), eternal separation from God in the lake of fire. The term "perdition" is related to the other descriptive words for the unsaved: the "lost" (Luke 19:10) and the "perishing" (I Cor. 1:18).

The author then expressed his confidence that both his readers and he were truly saved (10:39b). They were "them that believe," namely those who were justified and living by genuine faith. Their ultimate destiny was "the saving of the soul," the aspect of ultimate sanctification in which a person becomes totally conformed to Christ at His return. Justifying faith is a persevering faith.

Questions for Discussion

1. What causes faith to waver? How can it be corrected?

2. How can believers encourage each other? How can they increase their love for each other?

3. What presumptuous sins can believers commit today? How should they be warned? Rescued?

4. In what ways does God chastise sinning children? How does their judgment differ from that of the unsaved?

5. What is involved in genuine fear for God? How can it be fostered? How can it be balanced with a genuine love for God?

6. Are believers too interested in earthly possessions today? Is affluence harmful?

7. In what ways can a justified person live by faith? How can genuine salvation be detected?

11

The Nature of Faith
Hebrews 11:1-40

Within the Scriptures, Hebrews 11 is the classic chapter on faith. The noun ("faith") occurs twenty-four times in it, the adjective ("faithful") once, and the verb ("believe") once.

The need of the readers was faith and patient endurance. This chapter will cite a number of Old Testament characters who manifested their belief through such patience. The author wants his readers to follow their example (6:12).

I. DESCRIPTION OF FAITH (11:1-3)

The opening three verses contain a twofold description of the essence of genuine biblical faith, a general statement about the saints of the Old Testament era, and a declaration about creation.

A. Characteristics (11:1-2)

The principle of faith, not a specific act, is under discussion here. That is indicated by the fact that the noun "faith" occurs without the definite article "the" (*pistis*). Two features are given. First, faith is the "substance of things hoped for." The term "substance" (*hupostasis*) literally means "that which stands under anything." It earlier was used of the essence of the being of God (1:3) and of the basic trust of conversion (3:14). Here it is that confident assurance that future hopes will come to pass. It is not wishful thinking or emotional fantasy; rather, it has present confidence because it is placed in God who has promised and who will not lie. Hewitt stated, "Faith does not bestow reality on things which have no substance or reality in themselves."[1]

Second, it is the "evidence of things not seen." The term "evidence" (*elegchos*) is used only once elsewhere, translated as "reproof," one of the achievements of the inspired Scriptures (II Tim. 3:16). The verbal form (*elegchō*) is found often (John 8:46; 16:8; II Tim 4:2). It speaks of the ministry of the Holy Spirit whereby He brings about an inner awareness of the reality and truthfulness of nonmaterial entities. It is the inner conviction of the heart whereby one knows that God, heaven, hell, sin, and forgiveness are just as real as rocks and trees. Biblical faith fosters this intrinsic certainty.

The explanatory conjunction ("for") then shows that in the realm of this type of faith "the elders obtained a good report." They literally "were witnessed" (*emarturēthēsan*). They lived and made decisions within the domain of faith and their contemporaries watched them succeed. Beyond human observation God bore witness that their faith was genuine and that it demonstrated their justified position.

B. Creation (11:3)

Faith can look backward as well as forward. Belief about the past shares the same essence as belief about the future.

The author then stressed the conviction of himself and his readers about creation: "Through faith we understand. . . ." Genuine faith produces genuine knowledge. Christ claimed that the disposition of the will toward obedience would lead to a knowledge of spiritual doctrine (John 7:17).

The believer must accept the integrity and veracity of the biblical account of creation (Gen. 1-2). He denies the eternality of matter and believes that God brought the time-space

1. Thomas Hewitt, *The Epistle to the Hebrews* (Grand Rapids: Eerdmans, 1981), p. 171.

universe into existence out of the omnipotent expression of His decretive will. The phrase "the worlds" (*tous aiōnas*) literally translates as "the ages" (1:2). They were "framed" (*katērtisthai*), equipped or perfected, by a series of creative fiats (Gen. 1). From the present perspective of the writer, the material world ("things which are seen") was not made out of observable entities ("things which do appear"). The latter would include earth, water, and fire. Throughout the history of the world, pagan man has denied that the world of things had an instantaneous creation out of nothing. He has embraced the religion of antisupernaturalistic materialism. There conceivably could be here a reference to the molecular structure of living things, but the event of creation is probably expounded in this verse.

II. EXAMPLES OF FAITH (11:4–40)

This section has been appropriately called "The Hall of Fame of Faith." Here key men from Old Testament history are mentioned and extolled for their lives of faith and endurance.

A. Before the Patriarchs (11:4–7)

The first three men come from the period before the establishment of the Hebrew people. This era of history goes from basically the creation of man to the Flood (Gen. 1–11).

1. Abel (11:4)

Abel believed in God and demonstrated it by offering Him literally "a more sacrifice" (*pleiona thusian*).[2] His sacrifice was qualitatively superior to that of Cain. The same adjective is used of the righteousness which must exceed that of the scribes and Pharisees for entrance into the kingdom of God (Matt. 5:20). It is used of the gift of the widow's two mites which was "more" than the amount deposited by the rich (Luke 21:3). Cain brought

2. The adjective "excellent" is not in the text.

an offering of fruits and vegetables, but Abel brought "the firstlings of his flock" (Gen. 4:2–4). Beyond the observable, Abel gave out of a righteous heart sanctified by faith, whereas Cain was an evil person, influenced by Satan (I John 3:12). Abel knew that the remission of sins could only come through the shedding of blood. He undoubtedly perceived the significance of the death of the animals which provided the skins for the clothing of his parents after their sin (Gen. 3:21). The gift and offering of Abel have a message for all generations ("he being dead yet speaketh"). The lesson for the readers is that they might be killed by their unsaved Jewish brothers if they continue to trust in the sacrifice of Christ, the qualitatively better sacrifice which is the only one that God will accept.

2. Enoch (11:5–6)

Enoch did not die (Gen. 5:24). God took Enoch directly into heaven apart from physical death. Enoch's instantaneous transfer from earth to heaven was of the type living believers on earth will experience when Christ returns (I Cor. 15:51–53; I Thess. 4:13–18). The "testimony" or witness of Enoch was that "he pleased God." The Old Testament record claims that he "walked with God" (Gen. 5:22, 24). The example for the readers is that Christ might come for them in the midst of their afflictions. They should therefore walk in obedience and in anticipation of His imminent return.

It is impossible to please God apart from faith (11:6). Enoch, thus, was a justified person who walked with God by faith (10:38). The type of faith God honors must have two vital characteristics. First, the person who comes to God must believe "that He is." He naturally must accept the existence of God, but his belief must go beyond that fact. He must also affirm that God is all that He claims to be. The psalmist appropriately proclaimed this challenge from God: "Be still, and know that I am God" (Ps. 46:10). Second, the person who comes to God must also believe that God is a giving God, "a rewarder of them that diligently seek him." The act of seeking involves requests and patient endurance which originate with genuine faith. Faith asks, and faith will wait for answers (10:35–38).

3. Noah (11:7)

Noah's faith permeated three actions. First, he believed the warning about the universal flood, the outpouring of heavenly and subterranean water, namely "things not seen as yet" (11:1; Gen. 6:17). He knew it would happen. Second, Noah was "moved with fear" (*eulabētheis*), a devout reverence for the sovereign God. Such spiritual seriousness marked Christ (5:7), Simeon (Luke 2:25), and the men who buried Stephen (Acts 8:2). Third, Noah built the ark by faith.

Three results came from the construction, which was the patient endurance and evidence of Noah's faith. First, he saved his family. Second, he "condemned the world" in that his faith and message were rejected by his society.[3] He was a "preacher of righteousness" (II Peter 2:5). Third, he became an "heir of the righteousness which is by faith" along with Daniel and Job (Ezek. 14:14). Noah was just, perfect, and walked with God (Gen. 6:9).

B. The Patriarchs (11:8–22)

The key covenant which established the blessing of God upon both Israel and the world was made with Abraham and later reiterated to Isaac and Jacob. The history of this period covers the second half of Genesis (Gen. 12–50).

1. Abraham (11:8–10)

Abraham manifested his faith in three ways. First, he obeyed the call of God and moved from Ur of the Chaldees through the fertile crescent into Canaan, the land which God promised to him (11:8; Gen. 11:27–12:5). When he left his homeland, he did not know where he was going, but he believed God. His faith was the "evidence" of the unseen land (11:1).

---

3. The relative pronoun "which" (*hēs*) is feminine gender, agreeing with its antecedent "faith."

Second, Abraham "sojourned" (*parōikesen*) in the Promised Land (11:9). This verbal concept stresses a temporary dwelling in contrast to a permanent habitation (*katoikeō*). Contemporary believers are also characterized as such sojourners, foreigners, or strangers (Eph. 2:19; I Peter 1:17; 2:11). Abraham dwelt permanently in tents, and so did Isaac and Jacob. They endured the nomadic lifestyle in the very land given to them by God.

Third, Abraham looked with faithful anticipation to the eternal city which only God could build (11:10). He endured the temporary inconveniences of tent living in the hope that he would have a permanent residence in the holy city. The verb stresses constant looking throughout his lifetime.[4]

2. Sarah (11:11–12)

Both Abraham and Sarah were "old and well stricken in age" when God announced that they would become parents (Gen. 18:11). Sarah was ninety years old (Gen. 17:17). By faith, however, she received enablement to conceive, to carry the child to full term, and to bear the promised Isaac (11:11). Sarah's faith was not in herself or Abraham, but in a faithful God who promised. The record states, "And the LORD visited Sarah as he had said, and the LORD did unto Sarah as he had spoken" (Gen. 21:1).

Abraham was the "one" (*henos*)[5] who was "dead" or sexually sterile, yet he became the father of millions of physical descendants (11:12). He recognized the deadness of his body and of Sarah's womb, knew that it was humanly impossible, but believed that God would perform what He had promised (Rom. 4:19–21). God promised children as the stars and the sand (Gen. 22:17), so against human hope, Abraham "believed in hope" (Rom. 4:18).

3. All patriarchs (11:13–16)

The term "all" includes the three major patriarchs: Abraham, Isaac, and Jacob (11:9). Several qualities are attributed to them.

4. It is in the imperfect tense.
5. This numerical adjective is in the masculine gender.

First, they all died literally "according to faith" (*kata pistin*). Faith was the operative principle in their lives from the event of their justification to their respective deaths.

Second, the patriarchs did not receive the total fulfillment of the promises of God during their lifetimes.

Third, they saw their future realization by faith. Their faith epitomized its true essence (11:1).

Fourth, the patriarchs were "persuaded" that God would bring the promises to pass.

Fifth, they "embraced" the promises. They literally greeted or saluted them (*aspasamenoi*). Christ said to the Jews, "Your father Abraham rejoiced to see my day: and he saw it, and was glad" (John 8:56). They anticipated that one through whom God would keep His promise.

Sixth, the patriarchs confessed that they were earthly strangers and pilgrims and that they were citizens of the heavenly kingdom (Gen. 23:4).

Seventh, the patriarchs were seekers of the heavenly country, literally the "fatherland" (*patrida*) of the children of God (11:14). They were His patriots.

Eighth, they had no desire to return to Ur of the Chaldees even though they were pilgrims in Canaan (11:15). They did not draw back, but they endured in faith (10:38–39).

Ninth, the patriarchs desired the heavenly country which was better than either Canaan or Chaldea. The verb "desire" (*oregontai*) means "to covet, to reach out after, to stretch oneself toward, to aspire to." It is used of the believer who desires the office of pastor (I Tim. 3:1).

The result of their demonstrated faith is divine identification and preparation (11:16). God "is not ashamed to be called their God" and Christ is not ashamed to call them His brothers (2:11). God "has prepared for them a city," namely the Holy City which will be the eternal habitation of all saints (Rev. 21:2).

4. Abraham and Isaac (11:17–19)

The greatest test or trial of the faith of Abraham came when

188

God commanded him to kill Isaac as a sacrifice of obedience (Gen. 22:1-2). Abraham was the one who had received the covenant promises from God. He knew that Isaac was the unique son of promise; nevertheless, he was willing to trust God. The adjective "only begotten" (*monogenē*) literally means "one of a kind." Abraham had other sons by both Hagar and Keturah, but Isaac was special, the only son of Sarah.

Abraham knew that the covenant promises would go from him to Isaac (11:18). In the face of that truth, he still was willing to go through with the sacrifice.

Since Isaac was divinely promised and selected, Abraham believed that God would raise the boy from the realm of the dead ones (*ek nekrōn*). The patriarch fully intended to slay his son, but he also expected to witness the miracle of the resurrection. When he approached the place of sacrifice, he informed his servants: ". . .I and the lad will go yonder and worship, and come again to you" (Gen. 22:5). The verb ("come again") is in the plural in the Hebrew text; thus it can be translated, "We will come again." The only way for both of them to return would be the fact that Abraham believed that God would restore his son. He knew that Isaac had been conceived out of deadness. Thus, his birth was a "figure," a literal "parable" (*parabolēi*) of an anticipated resurrection.

The lesson for the readers was a challenge to their willingness to believe and to endure the tests of their day even though they knew that martyrdom might come to some of them, including their sons. Their hope of the resurrection, based upon the resurrection of Christ, would have to strengthen them.

5. *Isaac (11:20)*

Isaac, old and partially blind, blessed the younger son Jacob, thinking that the son was actually Esau (Gen. 27:28-29). He conferred financial prosperity, family supremacy, and the Abrahamic covenant promises upon him. In this sovereign control of a difficult situation, the will of God for Jacob was carried out (Gen. 25:23).

Later Isaac gave to Esau financial prosperity, temporary servitude of his family to that of Jacob, and an ultimate release from that subordinate position (Gen. 27:39–40).

Both blessings were accepted by faith, but the sons and the families had to wait for their fulfillment.

6. Jacob (11:21)

On his death bed, Jacob blessed Ephraim and Manasseh, the two sons of Joseph (Gen. 47:27—48:22). He worshiped God even though he had lived a difficult life and had not experienced all that God had promised.

In his blessing, Jacob expressed his faith about the future of Joseph's sons: "[Manasseh] shall become a people, and he also shall be great: but truly his younger brother shall be greater than he, and his seed shall become a multitude of nations" (Gen. 48:19).

7. Joseph (11:22)

Just before Joseph died at the age of 110, he predicted: "God will surely visit you, and bring you out of this land unto the land which he sware to Abraham, to Isaac, and to Jacob" (Gen. 50:24). He also asked that his bones be taken in the move and that they be buried in Canaan (Gen. 50:25). When the Exodus occurred about two hundred years later, Moses took the bones of Joseph (Exod. 13:19). They were carried during the forty years of wilderness wanderings. Subsequently, Joshua had them buried in Shechem, the parcel of ground Jacob had purchased (Josh. 24:32).

C. After the Patriarchs (11:23–31)

1. Moses (11:23–29)

Five statements are made about Moses' faith. First, his parents showed their faith in God by hiding their newborn for three months (11:23; Exod. 2:2; Acts 7:20). They were not afraid of the

THE NATURE OF FAITH

king's commandment that stipulated that all Jewish male babies should be cast into the Nile River (Exod. 1:22). Their faith caused them to endure the threat of imminent death. They perceived that Moses was a beautiful or goodly child (*asteion*). This adjective, used only twice in the New Testament and only of Moses, is translated as "proper" (11:23) and "exceeding fair" (Acts 7:20).

Second, when Moses became forty years old, Moses publicly identified himself as a Hebrew rather than the Egyptian son of the daughter of the Pharaoh (11:24; Exod. 2:11-15; Acts 7:23-28). The royal princess adopted the infant Moses after she found him in an ark by the side of the river (Exod. 2:1-10). She assigned the early childhood care of Moses to his natural mother, but she officially claimed him as her rightful son. The mother of Moses doubtless instructed him in his genuine ancestry. When Moses killed an Egyptian who was mistreating a Hebrew, he officially denied his Egyptian alignment.

Moses made a choice marked by faith (11:25). He chose "to suffer affliction with the people of God." The verb literally means "to have bad times with" (*sugkakoucheisthai*). He chose bad times over good times from the human perspective of financial enjoyment and security. If Moses had done nothing when he saw that Hebrew brother being abused, he could have enjoyed "the pleasures of sin for a season." The political and social advantages within the royal family of Egypt would have been pleasurable, but temporary. Sin does have its unique delights in this life.

Moses esteemed "the reproach of Christ greater riches than the treasures in Egypt" (11:26). He was reared to take his rightful position within the royal court. He became "learned in all the wisdom of the Egyptians, and was mighty in words and in deeds" (Acts 7:22). Since Egypt was the greatest power in that area of the world, Moses could have had anything he wanted. He, however, accepted "the reproach of Christ." What was this? Israel was the anointed, chosen nation and through her was to come the one who would bring to pass the covenant promises given to the patriarchs. By faith he anticipated the spiritual wealth of the heavenly kingdom. The verb "had respect" *(apeblepe)* literally translates "he was looking away from." He turned away from his earthly sight and utilized his spiritual vision to see by faith "the recompense," or reward, of faith.

Third, Moses forsook Egypt and fled into Midian (11:27; Exod. 2: 14-15; Acts 7:23-25). Fear of vengeance from the Pharaoh was not the real motivation behind his flight. For the next forty years of his life, he "endured, as seeing him who is invisible." The latter phrase denotes the sight of faith.

Fourth, he "kept the passover" (11:28; Exod. 12:1-28). By faith Moses personally obeyed God in the initial establishment of the Passover sacrifice. The families of Israel followed his instructions and likewise killed the lamb and sprinkled its blood upon the two side posts and the upper door post of each respective entrance (Exod. 12:7, 28). He believed that God would spare the firstborn of each family where the blood had been applied and that He would slay the firstborn of the Egyptians.

Fifth, the nation of Israel and Moses trusted God and passed through the waters of the parted Red Sea on the dry river bed (11:29; Exod. 14:21-31). They believed that the waters would not collapse upon them. The Egyptians, however, perished by drowning when they attempted to pursue the Israelites through the same passage.

2. Joshua (11:30)

How could Israel conquer the walled fortress of Jericho? God gave unusual instructions for the battle strategy, but Joshua and Israel believed Him. They were to march around the city once each day for six consecutive days. On the seventh day they were to march around the city seven times. After they had done this, Joshua charged the people to shout when they heard the sound of the trumpets (Josh. 6:1-20). When they shouted, the walls of the city fell flat. Their faith endured through that week of walking in circles. What they did humanly did not make sense, but they knew that God could be trusted, so they obeyed.

3. Rahab (11:31)

When the inhabitants of Jericho perished, the harlot Rahab was spared. She alone believed that God had given Canaan to the Israelites (Josh. 2:9-11). She confessed to the spies whom Joshua sent into the city: ". . .for the LORD your God, he is God in heaven above, and in earth beneath" (Josh. 2:11). James used Rahab as an illustration of a person who showed that she had faith by her works (James 2:25). She was justified by faith as evidenced by her works of faith. She subsequently married an Israelite and brought forth a son, Boaz, the husband of Ruth and the great-grandfather of David (Matt. 1:5-6). As a Gentile she blessed the descendants of Abraham; therefore she herself was blessed (Gen. 12:3; Josh. 2:12).

D. Various Saints (11:32-40)

This section summarizes the rest of Old Testament history, from the period of the judges through the kingdom era. Representatives are cited from the judges, the prophets, and the kings.

1. Their names (11:32)

The author believed that he had proved his premise ("And what shall I more say?"). God's people have always been called to endure patiently in faith. His examples were taken only out of the first six books of the Old Testament. There were many others, but he did not feel disposed to invest more writing time in that area ("for the time would fail me to tell").[6]

The author then quickly mentioned a few more names, hoping that the mere mention of those names would elicit the memory recall of their heroic deeds of faith. They were Gideon (Judg. 6-8), Barak (Judg. 4-5), Samson (Judg. 13-16), Jephthah (Judg. 11-12), David (I Sam. 16-30; II Sam. 1-24; I Kings 1-2), Samuel (I Sam. 1-16), and the prophets.

6. The participle "tell" (diēgoumenon) is in the masculine gender, thus the author had to be a male.

2. Their faith (11:33–34)

The saints mentioned above all accomplished something for God "through faith" (11:33a). Some subdued kingdoms, e.g., David (II Sam. 8), Gideon (Judg. 7), Barak (Judg. 4), Samson (Judg. 14), and Jephthah (Judg. 11).

Some wrought righteousness and produced national revival, e.g., Samuel (I Sam. 12:3–23; 15:33) and David (II Sam. 8:15).

Some, especially the prophets and kings, obtained promises and saw them fulfilled in their lifetimes (see Josh. 21:45; I Kings 8:56).

Others stopped the mouths of lions, e.g., Samson (Judg. 14:5–6), David (I Sam. 17:34–37), Benaiah (II Sam. 23:20), and Daniel (Dan. 6:22).

A few endured the violence of fire, e.g., Shadrach, Meshach, and Abednego in the fiery furnace (Dan. 3:25).

Some escaped the edge of the sword of their adversaries, e.g., Jephthah (Judg. 12:3), David (I Sam. 18:11; 19:10), Elijah (I Kings 19:1–2), and Elisha (II Kings 6:14–17).

Some out of weakness were made strong. Samson regained his power and destroyed his enemies (Judg. 16:28–30).

Others waxed valiant in fight, e.g., Barak (Judg. 4:14–15).

Some sent alien armies running.

3. Their endurance (11:35–38)

Some women saw their loved ones die, but then they "received their dead raised to life again." Two examples were the widow in the days of Elijah (I Kings 17:17–24) and the Shunammite woman in the time of Elisha (II Kings 4:17–35).

Others were "tortured" (*etumpanisthēsan*).[7] They were literally beaten to death. They did not accept deliverance through recanting and submission to error. They chose to die, knowing that they would obtain rewards for their faithfulness when they were resurrected (11:35b).

Others were tested through "mockings and scourgings" (11:36a). They were beaten with whips and rods. Hanani was one such example (II Chron. 16:10).

---

7. The type of drum called tympany is based upon this word.

Some experienced "bonds and imprisonment" (11:36b). Included in this group were Joseph (Gen. 39:20), Hanani (II Chron. 16:10), Micaiah (I Kings 22:26–27), and Jeremiah (Jer. 20:2; 37:15).

A few were stoned, as Zechariah the priest (II Chron. 24:20–22; Matt. 23:35).

Some were "sawn asunder." Tradition states that King Manasseh killed Isaiah in this manner. Amos reported that the Syrians did this to the inhabitants of Gilead (Amos 1:3).

Some were slain with the sword (I Kings 19:10; Jer. 26:23).

Some wandered in exile "in sheepskins and goatskins." They were outcasts with no enjoyment of material conveniences. They were "destitute, afflicted, tormented" (11:37b).

The author, awed by these saints' dedication of faith and unwavering endurance, then commented that they were too noble and grand to continue their existence on planet Earth. The "world was not worthy" to claim these saints as their own.

These tested saints wandered in deserts, mountains, dens, and caves of the earth (I Kings 18:4, 13). They were rejected strangers and pilgrims. Their lifestyles testified to the fact that their home was in heaven with God (11:38).

4. Their expectation (11:39–40)

All of these earthly rejects "obtained a good report through faith" (11:39a; cf. 11:2). They did not receive "the promise" in their lifetime. The promise includes all the blessings of the new covenant.

The reason for the delay was divine (11:40). Both the Old Testament people of God ("they") and the New Testament church ("us") share equally in the spiritual provisions of the death and resurrection of Jesus Christ, the mediator of the new covenant. They will both "be made perfect" (*teleiōthōsi*) in the first resurrection, the resurrection of the just of all ages. Together, they will enjoy the blessings of the incorruptible, immortal body in the kingdom of God which will be established on earth when Christ returns to the earth as King of Kings and Lord of Lords.

Questions for Discussion

1. What is the difference between biblical faith and mere human faith? Are there any similarities?

2. Can a Christian embrace evolution? If he does, does he deny the Genesis record and the meaning of faith?

3. How can faith be increased? Developed? Expressed?

4. Is there a difference between head and heart belief? What are the characteristics of each?

5. What attributes of the being of God must man accept by faith? What features about God does man find difficult to believe?

6. What contemporary trials of endurance are believers experiencing? Do Christians try to avoid trials?

7. Is evangelical affluence contradictory to the poverty of ancient saints? Does the world accept some of today's saints?

12

The Means of Encouragement
Hebrews 12:1–29

In this chapter the author continues to challenge his readers toward a life of faith and patient endurance. He uses a series of exhortations (12:1, 28)[1] and direct imperatives (12:3, 5, 12, 13, 14, 25)[2] to stimulate positive responses and spiritual advancement. The inferential conjunction ("wherefore") joins the two sections.

I. THE EXAMPLE OF CHRIST (12:1–2)

The previous chapter commended the acts of faith of various godly men. It is not wrong to follow the example of successful saints, but the ultimate standard for excellence must be the Savior. Paul wrote, "Be ye followers of me, even as I also am of Christ" (I Cor. 11:1). It is right to follow a human leader when that person is following the Lord. Christ often asked men to follow Him (Matt. 4:19).

A. The Appeal (12:1)

1. The exhortation

There is only one exhortation in this verse.[3] Its spiritual force

1. These are hortatory subjunctives ("Let us. . .").
2. These are in the imperative verbal mood, second person plural.
3. The text seems to have a second ("let us lay aside"), but it is actually a participle (*apothemenoi*).

is taken from the world of athletic games, the Greek and Roman Olympics. The Christian life is equated with a race to be run. Four features are stated about it. First, all believers are participants. The author included himself right along with his readers ("let us"). Paul often referred to the Christian experience as a race (I Cor. 9:24–26; Gal. 2:2; 5:7; Phil. 2:16).

Second, the command stresses persistent, daily running. It could be translated, "Let us keep on running" (trechōmen).[4] Christianity is not a spectator sport; it involves active participation. The length of the run directly corresponds to the years between conversion and death. The race is therefore more like a marathon than a dash.

Third, it must be done "with patience," the determination to finish in spite of pressures. This virtue can only be gained through tribulation (Rom. 5:3). God sovereignly provided the trial, and these believers needed to develop the ability to remain in the race under the duress of persecution (10:36).

Fourth, the course of the race was predetermined by God ("the race that is set before us"). The term "race" (agōna) transliterates as "agony." There is emotional, intellectual, physical, and spiritual agony in the will of God. It involves pain, exhaustion, and opposition. The race of each believer is distinctive; no two believers will experience the same trials. Although there are many similarities, yet there remain unique tests.

2. The basis

The success of the race is based upon a double awareness: an awareness of what others had done and a sensitivity of what each individual must do. This fact is indicated by two verbal participles: "having" (echontes) and "having put away from" (apothemenoi).[5] In the imagery of the amphitheater, the men of faith were seated as spectators, completely surrounding the circular track of Christian experience. They, however, were "witnesses" to divine faithfulness and to the blessings of faith and endurance. The readers could identify with their trials and

4. Present active subjunctive.
5. The KJV renders them respectively "seeing" and "let us lay aside."

know that they could likewise win over failure and discouragement.

The readers actively had to remove from themselves "every weight and the sin which doth so easily beset." Athletes could not run with excessive clothing or heavy shoes. In like manner, the believers had to shed the sin of unbelief and the encumbrances of self-pity and depression.

B. The Example (12:2)

The readers, like good runners, must look away from the distractions on either side, must not look backwards, and must set their sights on the finish line. The child of God must look toward his Lord and Savior, Jesus Christ. Christ is the "author" (*archēgon*) of faith. This title is translated elsewhere as "prince" (Acts 3:15; 5:31) and "captain" (2:10). It can mean that He is the ruler of faith or the originator of faith.[6] Christ is also "the finisher" (*teleiōten*).[7] On the cross, He both began and finished the soteriological work of redemption, propitiation, and reconciliation. He takes each believer from justification to glorification. Men are not only saved by Him, but also sustained.

Four praiseworthy features of Christ's victorious work are set forth. First, He was aware of "the joy that was set before him." The same verb (*prokeimai*) is used of the readers who have a race "set before" them and of Christ who had a joy "set before" Him. The "joy" was the anticipation of the salvation of lost men. Isaiah wrote, "He shall see of the travail of his soul, and shall be satisfied" (Isa. 53:11).

Second, Christ "endured the cross," the shameful death with its embarrassment, the pain, and the mockery. Since He endured the worst kind of death for His people, they should endure for Him.

Third, Christ was "despising the shame." The shame involved both what Christ suffered at the hands of men and what He experienced from God. It embraced the hours of darkness during which He was judicially separated from God.

6. The former is based upon the verb "to rule" (*archō*), whereas the latter stems from "to begin" (*archomai*).

7. This term is used only here in the New Testament.

Fourth, Christ triumphed in that He endured. He was rewarded with the exalted position at the right hand of God.

II. THE CHASTISEMENT OF GOD (12:3-11)

The classic treatment of chastisement is found in this portion of Scripture. The noun (*paideia*) is used four times (12:5, 7, 8, 11) and the verb (*paideuō*) is employed three times (12:6, 7, 10). Both terms are related to the Greek word for "child" (*paidion*). Chastisement, therefore, involves discipline and correction of the child of God through directive punishment and suffering. It is altogether different from the penal retribution of the unsaved.

A. Need of the Readers (12:3-5)

1. Consider Christ (12:3-4)

The imperative stresses serious, perceptive contemplation. It is a compound word with the literal translation "to reason up" (*analogisasthe*).[8] The English "analogy" is a transliteration of the Greek term. The readers are thus exhorted to construct a mental analogy of their trials with the sufferings of Christ on the cross. The Greek verb was also used in the fields of business and mathematics for adding up a column of figures. The challenge then was to work through the crucifixion experience, detail by detail, adding up all that Christ endured in order to provide salvation.

The Savior is described as the one "that endured such contradiction of sinners against himself." The term "contradiction" (*antilogian*) literally means "speech against." On the cross, He endured vocal ridicule against His integrity and redemptive intention. Concerning Christ's experience on the cross, Peter wrote:

> . . .because Christ also suffered for us, leaving us an example, that ye should follow his steps:
>
> Who did no sin, neither was guile found in his mouth:

8. The verb is used only here in the New Testament.

> Who, when he was reviled, reviled not again; when he suffered, he threatened not; but committed himself to him that judgeth righteously (I Peter 2:21–23).

Two results of this consideration are given. First, such positive thinking would eliminate mental and psychological discouragement (12:3b). Contemplation of self and adverse circumstances rather than a Christocentric outlook can cause a believer to "be wearied" (*kamēte*). This term is translated elsewhere as "sick" (James 5:15) and "hast . . . fainted" (Rev. 2:3). Mental depression can lead to psychological loss of determination and even physical fatigue and sickness.

Second, the readers should realize that they had not suffered to the same extent that Christ had (12:4). No one had yet died as a martyr for his faith ("unto blood"). The author however wanted the readers to know that martyrdom was a distinct future possibility ("not yet"). The verb "resisted" (*antikatestēte*) is a military term, meaning to stand in opposition against the enemy in the line of battle.[9] The participle "striving" (*antagōnizomenoi*) transliterates as "antagonistic." The word contains within it the term "race" (*agōna*) mentioned earlier (12:1). In attempting to run the race of the Christian life, the believer must contend with the taunts of his spiritual opponents. The "sin" of unbelief and quitting is personified as the real enemy. Of course, the temptation to fail came from the unregenerate Jewish establishment and the carnal believers as they imposed cultural and social pressure upon the readers.

2. Remember Scripture (12:5)

The opening words of this verse can be interpreted as either a declarative statement ("you have forgotten") or a question ("have you forgotten?"). Both are grammatically possible.

The "exhortation," taken from the proverbs of Solomon (Prov. 3:11–12), is an appeal to the children of the kingdom. It is actually individualized ("My son").

It contains two directives. First, "despise not the chastening

9. Used only here in the New Testament.

of the Lord." The command (*oligōrei*) is based upon the adjective "little" or "few" (*oligos*). To despise thus means to regard with small significance. The term "chastening" (*paideias*) is used for one of the purposes of the Scriptures in the "instruction [same word] in righteousness" (II Tim. 3:16). It is used of parents who should bring up their children in the "nurture [same word] and admonition of the Lord" (Eph. 6:4).

Second, neither "faint when thou art rebuked of him." The essence of rebuke occurs when God by His Spirit and Word brings about an inner consciousness of sin and guilt. Conviction is not synonymous with rejection; therefore a believer should not become discouraged when he is confronted with his wrongs. Rather, he should rejoice that he can correct the problem through confession, repentance, and growth.

B. Essence of Chastisement (12:6–8)

1. Its presence (12:6–7)

The presence of divine chastisement contains three assurances. First, it is a sign that the person is loved by God. It is clear that "whom the Lord loveth he chasteneth." Divine love desires the best for the object of that love. Moral development through tests and correction are necessary to produce conformity to righteousness in the will of God.

Second, it is an indication that the person has been received into the family of God. He "scourgeth every son whom he receiveth." There are no exceptions. In that culture to scourge (*mastigoi*) was to whip. The verb is used elsewhere of the scourgings of Christ by Pilate and the Roman soldiers (John 19:1).

Third, it is the evidence of the Father–son relationship (12:7). A believer must endure chastening and learn valuable spiritual lessons through its purpose. The verb "dealeth" (*prospheretai*) literally means "to bring toward." When God chastens, He wants to bring His child toward Himself, not away from His arms. Chastening is designed to promote love, understanding, and fellowship. Its essence is that of reciprocal attraction, not repulsion. In the natural realm, the chastisement of a son by a father is normal and is to be expected (12:7b).

2. Its absence (12:8)

All believers have become partakers of divine chastisement. If a professing believer lives apart from it, then he is actually a "bastard" (*nothoi*), an illegitimate child with no spiritual rights, privileges, or inheritance. Its absence is proof that he is not a son, one who will be brought to glory (2:10), one who has been redeemed (Gal. 4:5), and one who is an "heir of God through Christ" (Gal. 4:7).

C. Goals of Chastisement (12:9–11)

The conjunction "furthermore" (*eita*) joins the two sections and advances the argument for the necessity of chastisement. Three goals are set forth.

1. Respect of the Father (12:9)

The argument is based upon an analogy. In the human family, all could testify that their fathers "corrected" (*paideutas*) them. This is the same term, usually translated as "chastised." The response of the children to such discipline was the giving of "reverence" to the parent. The concept of reverence (*enetrepometha*) includes shame for the violation of parental will and the subsequent submission in recognition of the authority of the father. Paul used this verb, translated as "ashamed," to describe those who had rebelled against his authority (I Cor. 4:14; II Thess. 3:14; Titus 2:8). The term connotes an inward change of attitude and disposition of will.

In the family of God, believers should likewise respond by being "in subjection unto the Father of spirits."[10] The concept of subjection (*hupotagēsometha*) recognizes the chain of command and willingly accepts the position of subordination to God. In

10. These are human spirits (12:23).

this submission, a believer then can "live" the spiritual life to its maximum potential. In losing his life, he thus finds it (Matt. 16:25).

2. Personal profit (12:10)

Human chastisement has two features. First, it is temporary ("for a few days"). Second, many parents exercise it "after their own pleasure." A father sets up the boundaries within which he can tolerate the behavior of his child. Each parent is different in this respect; some are very strict, whereas others are liberal.

The purpose of divine chastisement, however, is for the "profit" of the believer. Only through obedience and submission can the children of God become "partakers of his holiness." The essence of holiness is separation from sin and a commitment to righteousness. This is the abundant life, the best of the believer's options.

3. Bearing of fruit (12:11)

The actual experience of going through chastisement does not "seem to be joyous." No child likes to be criticized, to suffer physically, to endure trials, and to be spanked. Enveloped by the discipline, the child can only perceive it as "grievous" (lupēs), full of psychological and physical pain.

When a person perceives the act of chastisement as an end in itself, and not as a means to an end, he fails to comprehend its true purpose. God wants the believer to become productive through the discipline. The child of God should yield "the peaceable fruit of righteousness." God is the spiritual husbandman who prunes and cleanses the believer so that the life of Christ will be manifested through him (John 15:1-5). It is "peaceable" in that the rebellious spirit has been changed into quiet submission and it is morally right. The only child of God who will produce this fruit is the one who is "exercised" by the chastisement. He willingly accepts it and learns by it; however, some harden themselves and are worse off as the result of the divine attempt to correct.

III. THE NECESSITY OF OBEDIENCE (12:12-17)

The inferential conjunction ("wherefore") introduces the conclusion to be derived from the lessons of chastisement. Positive action needed to be taken by the readers.

A. The Right Actions (12:12-14)

The readers were in a depressed state. They were like the Israelites at Kadesh-barnea right after they heard about the presence of giants in Canaan. Just as Joshua and Caleb tried to encourage the nation, so the author now strives to rally his readers around his leadership. Three commands are issued.

1. Straighten up (12:12)

This verse is taken from the cry of the prophet (Isa. 35:3; Job 4:3-4). The command "lift up" (*anorthōsate*) literally means "straighten up." The imagery is that of a man frozen with fear and anxiety. The hands "which hang down" (*pareimenas*) are literally hands "which remain beside the body in inactivity." The "feeble knees" are actually paralyzed (*paralelumena*). They were spiritually impotent. Just as Christ restored the paralytic to a normal walk by the power of His authoritative word, so the author wants his readers to get up from their position of spiritual immobility. The paralytic believed, and so they must believe.

2. Make straight paths (12:13)

The analogy of physical paralysis and healing to spiritual counterparts continues. A sense of proper direction is seen in the command. They should walk in a straight direction toward maturity in Christ. They should not be distracted by the persecutions and anxieties of life lest they fall into the ditch of unbelief and harm themselves spiritually. Just as Christ declared to the paralytic that his faith had made him whole, so these believers could be "healed" spiritually by a renewed faith manifested through endurance.

3. Follow (12:14)

Aggressive pursuit of peace and holiness should motivate the readers (Ps. 34:14; Rom. 14:19). The relative pronoun "which" (*hou*) refers to its antecedent "holiness" (*hagiasmon;* 12:10).[11] This is positional holiness or sanctification, imputed at the time of conversion (I Cor. 1:2, 30; 6:11; Heb. 10:10). The pursuit should be of the practical manifestation of that positional holiness.

B. The Wrong Attitudes (12:15)

The participle ("looking diligently"; *episkopountes*) relates back to the readers in their pursuit of peace and holiness. It literally means "oversight."[12] They needed to give serious supervision of their attitudes.

Three negative attitudes were to be avoided. First, a lack of appreciation and appropriation of the grace of God had to be watched (10:29). The verb "fail" (*husteron*) was used earlier in the warning to those who would seem "to come short" of the divine rest (4:1). Both justification and practical sanctification are achieved by the grace of God, not through a system of legalistic works and temple observances.

Second, the readers had to stop the "root of bitterness" from springing up within their spirits (Deut. 29:18). The verb "trouble" (*enochlei*) means "to crowd within." Without the preposition (*en*), it is used of demons who "vex" [same word] people (Luke 6:18; Acts 5:16). The imagery is of the root of bitterness springing up within the soil of the heart and crowding out the sense of thanksgiving.

Third, the defilement of the conscience had to be resisted. The verb indicates that which can stain or dye. Metaphysically it deals with moral defilement (Titus 1:15). Note the change from "any" to "many." The failure of one believer can have an adverse moral effect upon others.

11. Both are in the masculine gender.
12. The word "Episcopalian" is based upon it. It is frequently translated as "bishop" (I Tim. 3:2).

C. The Example of Failure (12:16–17)

The negative particle ("lest") introduces a specific illustration of a person who forfeited future spiritual privileges through a decision motivated by materialistic desires. Esau, in his encounters with Jacob and Isaac, was the classic example (Gen. 25:27–34; 27:26–40).

1. His sin (12:16)

Three aspects are cited. First, Esau was a "fornicator" (*pornos*). This term can refer to either spiritual or physical adultery. In the latter sense, it may embrace the taking of two Hittite wives by Esau (Gen. 26:34–35). Since the connective is "or" rather than "and," one could also argue that Esau was not morally evil.

Second, Esau was "profane" (*bebēlos*). He was thoroughly secularistic. This adjectival noun is based upon the Greek term for "threshold" (*bēlos*). A profane person thus metaphorically tramples on spiritual matters and treats them casually.

Third, Esau "sold his birthright" to Jacob for "one morsel of meat." The birthright privileges of the firstborn male included a double inheritance and family priestly leadership. He "despised his birthright" because he placed no value on spiritual blessings and responsibilities (Gen. 25:34). Esau thought that he was going to die from physical hunger. The warning to the readers was not to surrender their spiritual future for a moment of escape from physical persecutions.

2. His loss (12:17)

Before his death, Isaac wanted to bless Esau (Gen. 27:1–5). Apparently the father knew nothing of the sale of the birthright. Rebekah and Jacob then conspired to deceive Isaac and to steal the blessing (Gen. 27:6–30). When Esau came before Isaac to receive the blessing, he "was rejected" in that it was already given to Jacob. Esau then cried and wanted his father to reverse his decision to bless Jacob, but it was impossible. Esau "found no place of repentance" *within Isaac*. The decision was irrevocable.

In an earlier warning, the author cautioned that it was impossible to be renewed to repentance (6:6). A believer thus can make a decision to disobey God for materialistic reasons and find it impossible to reverse the future consequences of that willful act.

IV. THE TWO MOUNTAINS (12:18–24)

Here is a contrast between Sinai, the earthly mountain where the law was given, and Sion, the heavenly mount where the righteous dwell. Note the sharp comparison: "For ye are not come unto the mount. . . . But ye are come unto mount. . ." (12:18—22).

A. The Earthly Mountain (12:18–21)

The giving of the law at Sinai created a scene of terror, both in its observable characteristics and its emotional response within the witnesses.

1. Its objective description

The mountain could not be "touched" by man or beast (Exod. 19:12–25). Death was the penalty for willful disobedience or the accidental touch by an animal (12:20).

The mountain "burned with fire" at the time God descended upon it (Exod. 19:18). It was enveloped with "blackness and darkness," caused by a thick cloud that covered the mountain and by the smoke of the fire (Exod. 19:16, 18). There was a "tempest," a strong wind within the storm, accompanied by thunder, lightning, and an earthquake (Exod. 19:16, 18).

A trumpet sounded loudly and long (Exod. 19:16, 19). God then answered Moses by "a voice" (Exod. 19:19).

2. Its subjective response

The people asked that Moses speak to them rather than God directly speaking to them (12:19b; Exod. 20:19). When they saw the unusual phenomena, the Israelites backed away from the mountain (Exod. 20:18). Even Moses was frightened by the awesome display of divine power and holiness. All were repulsed by the scenario, not attracted to it.

In application, the law was designed to put forth the requirements of righteousness and to create an awareness of personal guilt and fear. It did not provide the gracious means to bring condemned sinners into the presence of God.

B. The Heavenly Mountain (12:22–24)

1. Its titles (12:22a)

First, it is called "Mount Sion." The earthly mount of Sion, or Zion, was the site of the city of Jerusalem (Matt. 21:5; John 12:15; Rom. 9:33; 11:26; I Peter 2:6). It personified the nation of Israel. This title, however, refers to the heavenly Sion where Christ presently dwells (Rev. 14:1).

Second, it is the "city of the living God." It is the great and Holy City, being prepared in heaven by Christ (John 14:2-3; Rev. 21:2, 10). Its composition and description are fully discussed by the apostle John (Rev. 21:10—22:5).

Third, it is the "heavenly Jerusalem." Just as earthly Jerusalem was the center of political and religious life for Israel, so the heavenly city is the seat of divine government and authority. In an allegory based upon the births of Ishmael and Isaac, Paul equated Sarah with the heavenly Jerusalem and the believers as the children of promise born out of divine grace (Gal. 4:19-31). Paul's theological argument was that it was impossible to be born of two different mothers (law and grace). The heavenly Jerusalem, therefore, is not populated with those who try to gain the favor of God through obedience to the Mosaic Law and sacrificial offerings.

2. Its inhabitants (12:22b–24)

The first group of inhabitants of Sion is literally "myriads of angels." The angels assisted in the giving of the law at Sinai (2:2; Deut. 33:2; Ps. 68:17; Gal 3:19). Today angels minister before the divine presence (Dan. 7:10).

The second group is "the general assembly and church of the firstborn, which are written in heaven." The term "firstborn" (*prōtotokōn*) is in the plural, designating all believers of the church age who have spiritual birthrights in Christ. The Savior is "the firstborn," the authoritative Head of the church, because He died and was the first to rise out of death (Col. 1:18). All names of genuine believers, who are heirs of God, are written down in the heavenly book of life (Luke 10:20; Phil. 4:3; Rev. 13:8; 20:12). The church is composed of saved Jews and Gentiles, called out of the world to constitute the family of God in the age between the crucifixion and the return of Christ (Matt. 16:18).

Third, God will be present at Mount Sion. He is "the God and judge of all."

Fourth, the Old Testament saints, designated as "the spirits of just men made perfect," will be present at Sion. They are judicially righteous before God because they trusted God for their salvation as Abraham did (Gen. 15:6). They are "made perfect" (*teteleiōmenōn*) in that they have received their new bodies through resurrection and have reached their heavenly destination (11:10, 13–16, 39–40).

Fifth, the Savior, namely Jesus, the mediator of the new covenant (8:6), is at Mount Sion. Christ promised His own that where He was, there they would be (John 14:3). The hope of the believer is to "ever be with the Lord" (I Thess. 4:17).

Sixth, the "blood of sprinkling," namely the blood shed by Christ on the cross, is on Mount Sion. There is a question as to whether the literal blood is there. It is more plausible to accept the view that the heavenly mountain has been made possible through Christ's redemptive work.

V. THE WARNING (12:25–29)

This section concludes with two appeals. The first is a direct imperative ("see"; 12:25), whereas the second is an inclusive exhortation ("let us have"; 12:28).

A. Beware (12:25–27)

The negative admonition reads: "Beware lest" (*blepete mē*). It is an appeal to constant vigilance and self-examination. The author did not want them to "refuse" God, the one who continues to speak to them through Christ and the authoritative New Testament (1:2; 12:24). The verb "refuse" (*paraiteomai*) was used of those who "made excuses" (same word) and rejected the invitation to attend the Great Supper (Luke 14:18–19). Careless disdain of a gracious request brought the loss of personal blessing.

Israel did not escape judgment when they rejected the divine message given at Sinai (12:25b; 2:2). Likewise, church believers under the new covenant will not escape divine chastisement if they casually neglect the message of Christ (12:25b; 2:3–4).

When God spoke at Sinai, His voice shook the earth (12:26a; Exod. 19:18). After God promised the new covenant to Israel, He predicted that He would shake the entire material universe (12:26b; Hag. 2:6). Any object of divine shaking is therefore temporary (12:27). In this category would be the earthly Jerusalem and sanctuary. Only unshaken things are eternal (12:27b). The heavenly mountain and city will remain forever.

B. Let Us Have Grace (12:28–29)

The eternal, heavenly, spiritual kingdom of God "cannot be moved." All believers are citizens of that country through the new covenant (Phil. 3:20).

For that possession ("receiving"), all believers should be eternally grateful. The exhortation stresses a constant maintenance ("let us have") of "grace." The essence of grace may be sustaining grace in the midst of trials (II Cor. 12:9), but it can also stress the concept of thanksgiving (Luke 6:32; I Tim. 1:12). The author later focused on the responsibility of the believer–priest to offer sacrifices of praise and thanksgiving (13:15–16).

When a believer becomes fully conscious that he is what he is by the grace of God and thanks God daily for His gifts, then he "can serve God acceptably with reverence and godly fear." God, who manifested fire at Sinai, will destroy the present universe with fire (II Peter 3:7, 10). Beyond this physical display of His power is the spiritual truth that God "is a consuming fire, even a jealous God" (Deut. 4:24).

Questions for Discussion

1. Why is unbelief an easy sin to commit? Can it ever be avoided? How can faith be developed?

2. Are Christians afraid to endure their crosses? Does contemporary culture influence impatience?

3. How can a believer mentally faint? Why are so many Christians emotionally weak? How can this situation be prevented?

4. What forms can chastisement take? Physical? Mental? Financial?

5. What positive values can come out of chastisement? In the human family? In the church?

6. What spiritual decisions are more crucial than others? Which are irreversible?

7. Do Christians believe that they can sin and get away with it? Where did they get this idea?

13

The Appeal for Separation
Hebrews 13:1-25

There is an abrupt change from the previous warning (12:25–29) to the closing exhortations of this chapter. No transitional word or phrase is given. The content moves quickly from the description of God as a consuming fire to the maintenance of brotherly love.

The analogy with the legalistic system of sacrifices, however, is not over (13:9–17). It remains the dominant thrust of the author's burden until the very end of the book.

I. SPIRITUAL QUALITIES (13:1-6)

In the midst of national crisis and cultural pressure, it can become easy to neglect social obligations and personal development of the Christian life. Here is a series of commands to bring the readers back to the basics of the faith.

A. Toward Others (13:1-3)

1. Love (13:1)

The first command is simple and direct: "Let brotherly love continue." The two English words ("brotherly love") are the translation of one Greek word (*philadelphia*). It obviously transliterates as "Philadelphia." The word refers specifically to the love of one Christian for his brother in the faith (Rom. 12:10; I Thess. 4:9; I Peter 1:22; 3:8; II Peter 1:7). It is never used biblically of natural love between children of the same parents or of a believer's love for the unsaved.

At conversion all believers are immediately implanted with a genuine love for God and for His children (I Thess. 4:9; I John 3:14; 4:19). That love, however, needs to be increased by the effort of each believer (10:24; I Thess. 4:9; II Peter 1:7). The readers possessed true brotherly love, a sign of their regeneration. The appeal is for its daily maintenance and proper manifestation (*menetō*).[1]

2. Hospitality (13:2)

Most people are naturally suspicious of strangers, especially those who knock on the front door of a private residence. Many houses are guarded by high fences, strong gates, watch dogs, and security systems. The doors have multiple locks on them. Such apprehension increases in the time of political and religious persecution.

The Jewish–Roman tension doubtless created the background for the second command: "Be not forgetful to entertain strangers." The imperative (*mē epilanthanesthe*) implies that the readers had stopped many acts of social benevolence.[2] The author wanted them to resume and to maintain their hospitality.

The infinitive phrase ("to entertain strangers") is actually the translation of an articular noun (*tēs philoxenias*). It is a compound word consisting of "love" and "strangers." A hospitable person therefore is one who loves strangers and who manifests it by providing food and lodging. All believers should be marked by hospitality (Rom. 12:13; I Peter 4:9). It is a qualification for a pastor (I Tim. 3:2; Titus 1:8).

Strangers may turn out to be blessings in disguise. They may be itinerant missionaries or pastors. The explanatory clause

1. Present active imperative.
2. The negative used with the present imperative means to stop doing what you have been doing.

("for") does not imply that the readers might possibly entertain angels in a human manifestation. Abraham, Sarah, and Lot on two separate occasions became gracious hosts to angels who conveyed divine messages to them (Gen. 18:1-8; 19:1-3). In like fashion, the readers could receive words of encouragement from saved household guests who were heretofore unknown to them.

3. Compassion (13:3)

To "remember" others is to uphold them in prayer, to have direct contact with them, and to help them in their affliction. Two groups of needy believers are mentioned. First, some were in prison ("in bonds"). The readers had to identify themselves with this group ("as bound with them").

The second group was composed of "them which suffer adversity." This term (*kakouchoumenōn*), translated earlier as "tormented" (11:37), refers to believers who were going through bad times—financially, physically, and socially. The reason for such remembrance was the fact that all believers are part of "the body," the true church of Jesus Christ (I Cor. 12:13). Paul wrote that all members of the body should suffer when one member is hurting (I Cor. 12:26).

Identification with fellow believers, either inside or outside the private residence, was an absolute moral necessity. The author wanted his readers to stand beside those Christians who were actively being persecuted for their faith and their identification with Christ.

B. Within Self (13:4-6)

1. Purity (13:4)

The opening two statements do not contain any verb. The indicative "is" (*estin*) could be supplied with this translation: "Marriage *is* honorable in all." The imperative (*estō*), however, could be inserted with this rendering: "Let marriage *be* honorable in all." Since other imperatives appear in the surrounding verses, the imperative seems to be more plausible.

Paul cautioned that the prohibition of marriage would be a mark of false teaching (I Tim. 4:3). Since the first three commands of this chapter dealt with personal commitments to others, there may have been a reluctance to enter into the permanent obligations of marriage. An imminent danger within this outlook is susceptibility to sexual temptation (I Cor. 7:1-2).

The author thus charged that marriage should be "honourable" (*timios*), a prized possession worthy of respect "in all" situations of life. It may be inadvisable to marry at times (I Cor. 7:25-26), but the institution and legality of marriage are always morally right. Sexual acts within the marital union are not sinful ("the bed undefiled"). Married believers must always meet the sexual needs of their partners (I Cor. 7:3-5).

God "will judge" the violators of proper sexual behavior, namely the fornicators (*pornous*) and the adulterers (*moichous*). The former term probably refers to premarital acts of sexual immorality committed by single men and women, whereas the second noun includes those who get involved in extramarital sexual affairs.

2. Contentment (13:5-6)

The reason why marriage and money are mentioned in the same context is that their abuse originates from the same cause of covetousness. Immorality and selfish greed stem from an evil desire to exploit others for one's own gratification. Quite often, wealth and wantonness are found together.

The term "conversation" (*tropos*) relates basically to the manner of behavior, the method whereby a lifestyle is shown to others. Again, a verbal imperative must be supplied ("let be"; *estō*). The phrase "without covetousness" is a translation of a triple compound Greek word (*aphilarguros*), literally meaning "no love of silver." It is used elsewhere only as a moral qualification of a pastoral candidate (I Tim. 3:3; "covetous").

The opposite of covetousness is contentment (*arkoumenoi*). Possessions, too few or too many, can cause a person to become depressed or arrogant (Prov. 30:8-9). Paul learned to be content in the midst of abundance or scarcity when he came to trust the sufficiency of God to meet his total needs (Phil. 4:10–13). In the midst of financial crisis, the believer must learn to give rather than to covet; then he will be in a position to receive divine sufficiency (II Cor. 9:8).

The presence of Christ is the greatest possession of the child of God (13:5b). The explanatory conjunction "for" (*gar*) intro-duces that fact. The next statement is extremely emphatic. It may be translated, "For He Himself has said: 'I will absolutely not leave you nor forsake you under any circumstances.' "[3] There are five negatives in this quotation (*ou mē . . . oud ou mē*). Only one is necessary to form a negation, but the usage of five should have given the readers firm encouragement (cf. Deut. 31:6, 8).

The results of the divine unconditional promise are intro-duced by the conjunction "so that" (*hōste*). There are basically two: confidence and peace (13:6). The author then boldly stated for his readers and himself the testimony of the psalmist (Ps. 118:6). Since God would help, there was no need to fear the inevitable persecution of men. Paul paraphrased this concept with his shout of triumph: "If God be for us, who can be against us?" (Rom. 8:31).

II. SPIRITUAL IDENTIFICATION (13:7–17)

Christians are encouraged to follow the example of other believers and of the Lord (I Cor. 11:1; I Tim. 4:12; I Peter 2:21). In this section the author challenged his readers to imitate their leaders and their Savior.

A. With Their Leaders (13:7–9)

The pastors are identified as those who "rule" (*hēgeomai;* 13:7, 17, 24). The term indicates men who are held with high esteem

3. Leaving implies the withdrawal of support, whereas forsaking indicates the separation of personal presence.

(Phil. 2:3; I Thess. 5:13). It is also translated as "Governor" (Matt. 2:6). Their sphere of spiritual administration included the readers ("over you").

1. Marks of true leadership (13:7)

Three marks of leadership are given. First, the leaders authoritatively proclaimed biblical truth. The verb ("have spoken") may indicate that these leaders had already died.[4] They could have possibly been that first generation of preachers who actually witnessed the earthly ministry of Christ (2:3). The past tense of the verb, however, may indicate their ministry only up to the time of the writing of the book.

Second, these leaders were men of faith ("whose faith"). The verb "follow" (*mimeisthe*) can be transliterated as "mimic." The readers were to imitate the leaders' attitudes and acts of faith in the midst of tribulation.

Third, their Christian lifestyle manifested endurance and victory. The term "end" (*ekbasin*) is used only once elsewhere. It is "the way of escape" which God provides to believers when they are going through difficult temptations (I Cor. 10:13). These leaders, therefore, showed how enduring faith could triumph. They were living examples of the way of faith pioneered by the Old Testament characters (chap. 11).

2. The ultimate leader (13:8)

Jesus Christ is immutable (Mal. 3:6). He is "the same yesterday, and to day, and for ever." Church leaders can come and go, but the living Head of the church is ever present. Pastors can fail, but Christ never disappoints.

Although the readers could follow the faith of their leaders, they should never place their faith in the leaders themselves. Their trust should always rest in the unchanging Savior. Immutability is an attribute of the divine nature which God innately possesses.

4. This view is held by Thomas Hewitt, *The Epistle to the Hebrews* (Grand Rapids: Eerdmans, 1981), p. 207.

Although Christ never changes, His program can and does. In His earthly ministry Christ commanded the apostles to preach to Jewish people only (Matt. 10:5–6), but after His resurrection He commissioned them to evangelize all nations (Matt. 28:18–20). Christ's person is immutable, but His program is not immobile.

3. Marks of false leadership (13:9)

The person and redemptive work of Christ form the foundation of the Christian system of orthodox doctrine (II John 9). All teaching and all teachers must be evaluated by proper biblical christology. Based upon that axiom, the author cautioned his readers ("Be not carried about").

Three aspects of error are set forth. First, false leaders promote false doctrine. The adjective "divers" (*poikilais*) shows that error can take on many forms, whereas Christian truth is always singular. There is a unity within biblical truth (Eph. 4:4–6). The other adjective ("strange") indicates that false teaching has its origin and essence from without the inspired Word of God. In speaking of the apostates, John observed: "They are of the world: therefore speak they of the world, and the world heareth them" (I John 4:5). Christ warned His disciples, or sheep, about heeding the voice of a stranger (John 10:5).

Second, false teachers emphasize externals. Spirituality is not caused or maintained by dietary regulations in compliance with the Levitical code ("not with meats"). Christ criticized the hypocritical Pharisees for their emphasis on traditionalism and outward appearance (Matt. 15:17–20). Paul warned the churches about the Judiazers who tried to impose faulty prohibitions (Rom. 14:2, 14, 21; Col. 2:8, 16–23). The right condition of the heart is secured by grace.

Third, false teaching produces no effective spiritual results ("have not profited them that have been occupied therein"). False teachers could not impart justification, sanctification, or fellowship with God.

B. With Jesus Christ (13:10-16)

1. The altar and food (13:10-11)

The unsaved Jews charged that the Jewish believers had no temple, no sacrifice, and no priest. The author, however, repudiated that false accusation.

All believers "have an altar," namely the cross of Jesus Christ. The unsaved priests who "serve the tabernacle" have "no right to eat" of that altar. In the sermon on the Bread of Life, Christ invited the multitudes to eat His flesh and to drink His blood. In so doing, they would live forever (John 6:51-58). His life could become theirs by accepting Him by faith (John 6:63). Spiritual life and growth come from Him.

On the Day of Atonement the bodies of the sacrificial beasts were burned outside of the camp of Israel (13:11; Lev. 4:12, 21; 16:27). Only the blood was taken into the Most Holy Place and sprinkled on the mercy seat by the high priest. No one ate the flesh or drank the blood of that national sin offering. The believer thus has a greater participation in the essence of the sacrificial system by his assimilation of the total life of Christ, who made the perfect propitiatory sacrifice.

2. The reproach and the city (13:12-14)

Christ sanctified His people with His own blood (10:10). He positionally set them apart from the dominion of sin unto Himself. He "suffered without the gate" in that He died on Golgotha, a hill outside the city walls of Jerusalem. The Jewish leaders and the Roman officials rejected Him; therefore they took Him out of the city and crucified Him.

The exhortation appeals for an identification with the historical Savior: "Let us go forth therefore unto him without the camp" (13:13). This is a call for both a spiritual and a geographical movement. The "camp" is a reference to the actual city of Jerusalem. As Jewish-Roman tension mounted, the appeal to patriotism caused Jews to remain within the city and to defend both it and the temple. To leave the city would bring charges of cowardice and treason. The author, nevertheless, wanted the believing Jews to disassociate themselves from the earthly city. Just as Christ was paraded outside the city in public ridicule and disgrace (Luke 23:35–37), they should be willing to exit the city "bearing his reproach." They must gladly carry the offense of the cross as He bore the cross for them.

The explanatory conjunction ("for") gives the reason for the departure (13:14). The Jewish Christian does not have in this life a "continuing city." Christ predicted that the city of Jerusalem and the second temple would be destroyed (Matt. 22:7; 24:1–2). Daniel prophesied that the Romans would "destroy the city and the sanctuary" after the death of the Messiah (Dan. 9:26). Any city built by man is temporal. The Christian should seek the heavenly city, the "one to come," the city of the living God (11:10; 12:22).

3. The spiritual sacrifices (13:15–16)

The nation of Israel had a priesthood which offered sacrifices in behalf of the people. All believers, however, are spiritual priests. They are a holy and royal priesthood under obligation "to offer up spiritual sacrifices, acceptable to God by Jesus Christ" (I Peter 2:5, 9). King David, unable to be a Jewish priest, still perceived his ability to offer spiritual sacrifices unto God (Ps. 51:17, 54:6).

The believer–priest can go before God through Christ ("by Him"). He can offer two types of sacrifices. The first consists of "praise to God," the act of worshiping God for the sake of His being alone. A believer praises God when He acknowledges God to be what He really is. It is primarily an appreciation of the Giver, and secondarily of His gifts. The verb "giving thanks" (*homologountōn*) can literally be translated "confessing." As the "fruit of lips," it must embrace the vocal expression. A believer must orally tell God how much he loves and appreciates Him.

The second type of sacrifice refers to benevolence toward men (13:16). The two English infinitives ("to do good and to communicate") are actually translations of two nouns (*tes eupoiias kai koinōnias*).[5] The first word ("good deeds") emphasizes the

5. The two nouns appear with a single article; thus, they reveal two aspects of a single act.

involvement of time and effort whereas the second term ("sharing") points to the giving of money, clothing, and other material
goods.

The author notes that "with such sacrifices God is well pleased."
These are sweet-smelling offerings, given voluntarily out of love.
The sacrifices of believers are not limited to these types. One can
offer his total self to live in the will of God (Rom. 12:1; II Cor.
8:5).

C. With Their Leaders (13:17)

1. The commands

Two commands are given. First, the readers are charged to
"obey them that have the rule over you." Although all believers,
as priests, have positional oneness in Christ and equal access
into the presence of the Father, there is still a functional order
of leadership and authority within the local church. The verb
(*peithesthe*) conveys the idea of inner persuasion of the authoritative right of the pastor and a willing compliance to follow such
leadership.

Second, the readers are to "submit [themselves]." There must
be voluntary subordination, joined by a desire to do what the
leaders suggest.

2. The reasons

Four reasons for obedience to leaders can be seen. They are
given from the perspective of the leader. First, pastors have a
divinely given responsibility to "watch" over their congrega-
tions. The verb (*agrupnousin*) always occurs elsewhere with the
action of prayer (Mark 13:33; Luke 21:36; Eph. 6:18). It connotes
a mental and spiritual sensitivity toward moral danger. Pastors
must carefully supervise the moral and doctrinal health of their
spiritual flocks.

Second, pastors will have to "give account" of their stewardship. After all, the believers are really the sheep of Christ (John
21:15–17; I Peter 5:2). The pastors' leadership gifts and opportu-

nities were bestowed upon them; therefore they will render a record of their service at the judgment seat of Christ (II Cor. 5:10).

Third, pastors want to execute their ministry "with joy and not with grief." Obedient children are always a cause of rejoicing to their parents, whereas rebellious sons and daughters produce heartache. John said: "I have no greater joy than to hear that my children walk in truth" (III John 4).

Fourth, insubordination is actually "unprofitable" for rebels. The term (*alusiteles*) has a unique derivation.[6] It is composed of three concepts: "not" (*a*) and "loose" (*luō*) and "tax" (*teles*). A rebel does not get away with his insubordination even though he does not pay his obligation to his human leader. He is not loosed from his spiritual tax toward God. God will require it of him, either in this life or at the judgment seat (I Tim. 5:24).

III. CLOSING CONCERNS (13:18–25)

Hebrews closes like a typical epistle, with personal remarks and the usage of the first person personal pronoun ("I").

A. Prayer (13:18–19)

The author asked his readers to pray for him. The plural ("us") may be an editorial device or it may include the author and his associates, perhaps Timothy (13:23). Two concerns are set before them.

1. His integrity (13:18)

The author was persuaded ("we trust," *pepoithamen*) that his life was right in three areas. First, he was convinced that he had a "good conscience" before God and toward men. A good conscience is always reinforced by a cleansed heart and an unhypocritical faith (I Tim. 1:5). He was unaware of any unconfessed sin in his life.

6. Used only here in the New Testament.

Second, the author believed that he had a submissive will ("in all things willing"). His motivations were pure. He wanted to do the will of God. He was not insubordinate toward the highest authority of a believer.

Third, the author's goals were correct. He desired "to live honestly." His aim was to have behavior consistent with the glory of God.

The author thus wanted his readers to pray that he would maintain these qualities of spiritual integrity and leadership.

2. His restoration (13:19)

The author also besought his readers to pray that he might be restored to them. He either was in prison or at some consid- erable distance from them. God can use the intercession of concerned believers to effect the release of His imprisoned children (Philem. 22).

B. Benediction (13:20–21)

The author then made an appeal to God who is described in two ways. First, He is "the God of peace." As such, He can give peace that passes all human understanding and calms anxious hearts (Phil. 4:7, 9). In their distress and confusion the readers needed a fresh perception of their God.

Second, He is the one who resurrected Christ. The verb "brought again" (*anagagōn*) means "to lead up" (Rom. 10:7). God led Christ up out of the realm of the dead ones, out of sheol or hades, out of the place of comfort (Luke 16:19–31; Acts 2:27).

1. God and Christ (13:20)

Christ is called the "great shepherd of the sheep." Elsewhere He calls Himself "the good shepherd" who lays down His life for the sheep (John 10:11). Peter identified Him as the "chief shepherd," who would reward the shepherd–pastors of local churches (I Peter 5:4). Since the psalmist declared that Jehovah was the Shepherd of believers, then Christ must also be divine, equal to the Father and Spirit within the Trinitarian oneness of the eternal being (Ps. 23:1).

The shepherd–sheep relationship was established at the cross "through the blood of the everlasting covenant." The new covenant thus is everlasting, whereas the old covenant of law only extended from Moses to Christ, from Sinai to Calvary (Luke 22:20).

2. God and the believer (13:21)

The author desired that God "perfects" (*katartisai*) every believer. This term was used by the pagan Greeks for the setting of broken bones. It was also employed for the mending of the nets of fishermen (Matt. 4:21). The readers thus had some spiritual fractures and rips that only God could repair. God performs this task through the perfecting ministry of pastor-teachers who faithfully proclaim the inspired Word (Eph. 4:12; II Tim. 3:16–17).

Five features of perfection are given. First, its sphere is "in every good work." People must be doing works that correspond to divine goodness. God cannot perfect a person when he willfully chooses to disobey revealed directives.

Second, perfection's goal is "to do the will of God." Perfection leads toward performance.

Third, the energy of perfection comes from God. He is the one "working in you that which is well pleasing in his sight." After Paul charged the Philippians to work out their own salvation, he then explained, "For it is God which worketh in you both to will and to do of his good pleasure" (Phil. 2:13).

Fourth, the means of perfection is "through Jesus Christ."

Fifth, the ultimate end of perfection is the glory of God ("to whom be glory forever and ever"). To glorify Christ is to glorify God.

C. Closing Remarks (13:22–25)

1. About the letter (13:22)

The author then besought the readers to "suffer the word of exhortation." The verb (*anechesthe*) is often translated as "to forbear" (Eph. 4:2; Col. 3:13). The author is using a soft approach. He wants his readers to receive the admonitions of the book even though they irritate their faulty theological concepts. The terms "beseech" (*parakalō*) and "exhortation" (*paraklēseōs*) are built on the same stem.

The author then claimed that he had written his letter "in few words" (*dia bracheōn*). The epistle, however, is not brief when it is compared with the other New Testament letters. It is short though, because much more could have been penned to show the superiority of Jesus Christ and the new covenant.

2. About Timothy (13:23)

The author then informed the readers that Timothy had been "set at liberty" (*apolelumenon*). No epistle records an imprisonment for Timothy, but he could have been placed in jail or under house arrest after he received his two epistles from Paul.

The author expressed hope that he would come with Timothy to the home of the readers.

3. About salutations (13:24–25)

The author then asked his readers to relay his salutation to their pastoral leaders and to all the saints in that region.

The next salutation is intriguing: "They of Italy salute you." This statement may indicate that the author was in Italy at the time of writing or that Italian believers were with him. Either view is acceptable grammatically.

Finally the author extended his personal blessing to them: "Grace be with you all."

Questions for Discussion

1. Are Christians hospitable today? What influences can rob believers of opening their homes?

2. Why do some Christian marriages fail? What can be done to prevent immorality and divorce?

3. Are believers greedy today? Is affluence a help or hindrance to the godly life?

4. Do believers respect their pastors? Do they willingly obey the leadership within a local church?

5. In what ways can a believer bear the reproach of Christ? Why do some fail to bear the cross?

6. What is involved in genuine praise? Thanksgiving? Benevolence? Can the difference between the real and the hypocritical be detected by man?

7. Do believers suffer rebuke aimed at them? Should the pulpit criticize the pew? Defend your answer.

Selected Bibliography

Bruce, F. F. *The Epistle to the Hebrews.* Grand Rapids: Wm. B. Eerdmans Publishing Co., 1981.

Hewitt, Thomas. *The Epistle to the Hebrews.* Grand Rapids: Wm. B. Eerdmans Publishing Co., 1981.

Hughes, Philip Edgcumbe. *A Commentary on the Epistle to the Hebrews.* Grand Rapids: Wm. B. Eerdmans Publishing Co., 1977.

Kent, Homer A. *The Epistle to the Hebrews.* Grand Rapids: Baker Book House, 1983.

Kistemaker, Simon J. *Hebrews.* Grand Rapids: Baker Book House, 1984.

MacArthur, John. *Hebrews.* Chicago: Moody Press, 1983.

Newell, William R. *Hebrews: Verse by Verse.* Chicago: Moody Press, 1978.

Robertson, Archibald Thomas. *Word Pictures in the New Testament.* Vol. V. Nashville: Broadman Press, 1932.

Ross, Robert W. "Hebrews," *The Wycliffe Bible Commentary,* Charles F. Pfeiffer and Everett F. Harrison, eds. Chicago: Moody Press, 1963.

Wiersbe, Warren W. *Be Confident.* Wheaton: Victor Books, 1982.